COMMUNICATION AND DEVELOPMENT

A Study of Two Indian Villages

BY Y. V. LAKSHMANA RAO

UNIVERSITY OF MINNESOTA PRESS

Minneapolis

© Copyright 1966 by the University of Minnesota
ALL RIGHTS RESERVED

Printed in the United States of America at
the Lund Press, Inc., Minneapolis

Library of Congress Catalog Card Number: 66-21940

PUBLISHED IN GREAT BRITAIN BY THE OXFORD UNIVERSITY PRESS, LONDON,
AND IN CANADA BY THE COPP CLARK PUBLISHING CO. LIMITED, TORONTO

TO

Ammani

MY FRIEND, WHO ALSO HAPPENS TO BE

MY MOTHER

ACKNOWLEDGMENTS

THE theoretical backdrop of this study is in itself testimony to the debt I owe Professor Wilbur Schramm. I would like to add, however, that the help he gave me was not all theoretical; a great deal of it was practical, offered with warmth and generosity during my stay at the Institute of Communication, Stanford University. (Dr. Schramm's latest book, *Mass Media and National Development* (Stanford, Calif.: Stanford University Press and Paris: UNESCO, 1964), is not specifically referred to in these pages because of the timing of its publication. For an over-all view of the subject matter discussed in these pages, however, there is no better reference.)

For my initiation into the broader field of communication and for showing me the way toward new horizons, Professor Raymond B. Nixon was largely responsible. I take this opportunity to thank him for the stimulating and delightful years I spent with him at the School of Journalism, University of Minnesota. It was there that I also came to know and benefit from association with Professors Roy E. Carter, Jr., and Robert L. Jones. My debt to these three specifically and to the rest of the warmhearted faculty of Murphy Hall is truly unquantifiable.

This book is dedicated to my mother, but not merely for the usual reason. Her invaluable help, which extended into all phases of the field work reported in this study, was given with love, affection, and pride. Even if I were to attempt to return it in kind, she would be shortchanged. So would my wife, Bhashi, whose enthusiastic encouragement was given in the midst of her own demanding doctoral program; but for her this report would not have received the close scrutiny which only an intelligent woman's intuition can supply. Finally (but with no conscious ordinal scaling) the help I received from my dear friend Elizabeth Closs has been both substantive and indefinable. I can only acknowledge it.

In revision of the manuscript, I have received excellent advice from two persons. Satish Arora went over it with me page by page and donated countless hours of his valuable time; so did Jeanne Sinnen, without whose methodical and sharp blue pencil this manuscript would not have achieved its present final form. For any blemishes that may still remain, the blame, of course, belongs to the author — and the credit to the reader for noticing them.

For the very essential help which I received at the proof and indexing stage, I thank Susan Loppert and Sheila Melville.

To the many friends we made in Pathuru and Kothuru, this report may be totally unintelligible. However, without their generous hospitality and cooperation, it could not have been written.

Y. V. L. R.

September 1965

TABLE OF CONTENTS

Communication and Development

CHAPTER I

INTRODUCTION

ERRANNA is an illiterate, sixty-two years old, one of the Gaondla caste whose members traditionally depend for their livelihood on the tapping of palm trees and the selling of the fermented juice (*kallu*). He has spent all his life in a virtually isolated village, twenty-five miles from Hyderabad, the capital of Andhra Pradesh in South India.

Rajayya is a forty-one-year-old member of the Brahmin priest caste. He is a high school teacher in a village connected directly by rail and road to Visakhapatnam, fourteen miles away. This city is the seat of the Andhra University and a busy seaport. Rajayya has had four years of college and has traveled extensively.

Knowing this much about them, one might make certain predictions: Rajayya will be well informed about public affairs—the national development programs and the like. Erranna will be quite ignorant about them, indeed uninterested in such things as the five-year plans and nuclear explosions. Rajayya will seek information,

3

meet people, discuss news, give advice, and generally conduct himself in such a way that he will be a respected member of the community. Erranna, on the other hand, will be content with his traditional occupation, will be conscious of his place in the community and will generally confine himself to association with lower-caste groups, will work hard during the day and sleep soundly during the night. His position in the community will limit his circle of friends to those who are as illiterate and as ill informed as he is.

These are the differences which caste and education make — or at least so one might understandably assume.

But is this indeed the case with Rajayya and Erranna? Are they really as described here? No. The truth is almost the opposite. It is Erranna who has heard of the "poisoned air" (radioactivity) released by Russia's testing of the "Big Bomb" and its possible dangers, of life insurance, of the "Goa War," and so on. Rajayya, on the other hand, can only make a vague guess that exploding a bomb is bad because "a bomb kills people." It is Erranna who is a respected member of his community, because he is well informed, cosmopolitan in his outlook, sociable, jovial, a fine conversationalist, and a modest person. Rajayya is seldom stopped on the road because there are few who wish to talk to him; he isolates himself in his house and interacts with neither his students nor their parents ("I have nothing in common with them"). He claims that he reads the newspaper every day and takes part in the preparation of a news bulletin which is read out at the morning assembly in school, but he has not heard of the deliberations of a commission inquiring into the sharing of river waters between Andhra and two adjoining states, although the activities of the commission made lead stories for five consecutive days in all the newspapers circulating in the village.

Erranna and Rajayya are *not* typical members of their respective communities in their approach to life, their information level, and their view of the future. But they are typical in some other respects: their way of dress and certain behavioral patterns.

Erranna dresses in the style of the traditional South Indian villager—he wears a *dhoti* topped by a loose collarless shirt, over which a handspun blanket is draped for comfort in the winter. On

4

his feet are two strong, thick, crudely finished slippers. Rajayya wears what could pass for a Western costume — a pair of cotton trousers, a plain "bush shirt," and shoes. It is true that Rajayya is in the minority in his village, but almost every educated man who has been exposed to some city influence would wear such a costume there, whereas in Erranna's community even the richest landlord who spends half the year in the city dresses more or less like Erranna. Rajayya's house has cemented floors, a few chairs and cots, and at least two tables, while Erranna lives in a small tiled house with mud floors and no furniture. Erranna rarely, if ever, goes to the local teashop, but Rajayya eats his lunch fairly regularly at a restaurant.

In pointing out this seeming paradox of the informed illiterate and the ignorant literate, of the use of illiteracy and the misuse of literacy, my intention is to stress at the outset the complicated nature of the kind of field study reported here, a study of the influence of communication on development in a "developing" nation. An investigator looking for communication channels or trying to reach general conclusions about the communication patterns within communities can depend on raw data only up to a point and no further. Even if individual communities are studied intensively, the significant differences in personalities in the same social structure can often make the exceptions more important than the rule.

Erranna and Rajayya will appear in later chapters; so will many others. Often they will be anonymous units in a mass; but often too they will be singled out. For it is important that we not lose sight of some of the individuals who play such important roles in the process of communication.

Purpose and Nature of the Study

In exposing himself to the growing literature on "underdeveloped" and "developing" countries, a person coming from one of these countries cannot but be troubled by statements such as this: "A great economic, social and political transformation is sweeping the underdeveloped countries. This transformation is manifested in new aspirations and expectations, a new eagerness to plan and promote economic growth and to acquire modern technology, a challenging of age-old traditions, the rise to power of new leaders, and the emergence of new nations."[1] One immediate reaction to such a statement may be: "Why is this not so in my country?" Perhaps, to some extent, it is, but how far down has this "sweeping transformation" actually gone? Doubt arises, even if one is generous enough to treat such statements as well-meant and optimistic hopes of sympathetic observers. In any case, they do serve a useful function. They stimulate one to inquire a little further.

To a student of communication, the inquiry takes on greater significance, for a developing nation like India, say, in contrast to a nation like the United States, has a very large percentage of illiteracy and a very low per capita income. Under such conditions, how do people inform themselves enough to take part not only in the political system but also in the country's total effort at development? The logical question then becomes: "To what extent are the two related — development and communication?"

That is the question I am exploring in these pages. Since India is the developing nation I know best, it provided the setting for my field study.

I began the study with two assumptions: first, that while India has developed in several areas the rate of progress has been slower than it might have been; second, that communication is a significant factor in development. The proposition for the study, based on these two assumptions, is that communication plays a significant role in national development and that the relationship between communication and development is a constant and cumulative one.

"Communication," as used here, refers to a social process — the flow of information, the circulation of knowledge and ideas in human society, the propagation and internalization of thoughts. It does not refer to electronics, roads and railways, or vehicles.

It is through communication that people can learn about new

[1] Eugene Staley, *The Future of Underdeveloped Countries* (New York: Frederick A. Praeger, 1961), p. xiii. It seems only fair to add that this passage is quoted merely as an illustration. Similar statements can be found in innumerable prefaces, especially to studies pertaining to the developing countries.

ideas, can be stimulated by change which is conveyed to them or be cognizant of change and what it means, and can understand what is going on around them. They should be conscious of the "fourth dimension" — that which is going on around an individual in which he may not be directly involved — for only then can they actively participate in the development process when the opportunity presents itself. If one is not conscious of what is going on outside his immediate world the opportunity itself will not be recognized. For any development to take place, opportunity must be seized (and often created) by a large number of people in any given community. Otherwise development remains lopsided and the fruits of growth are not shared.

"Development," as used here, refers to the complicated pattern of economic, social, and political changes that take place in a community as it progresses from a traditional to a modern status. These changes include political consciousness, urbanization, division of labor, industrialization, mobility, literacy, media consumption, and a broad general participation in nation-building activities.

While some of the factors that are relevant in any investigation of national growth may be amenable to measurement with the tools available now (e.g., literacy, urbanization, media consumption), others are not. Some generalizations can be made, but only guardedly. Some elements can be isolated, others cannot. As Robert Redfield has put it, "The effort of the scientific mind to reduce the reality to elements amenable to analysis, comparison, and even mensuration early results in a distortion or in the disappearance of the subject matter as common sense knows it." [2] This is not the place to go into a discussion of the "holistic" nature of human communities. It must suffice to point out that although the whole may be equal to the sum of the parts, still it is difficult to comprehend the whole or to know each of the parts. Any such approach as mine here must necessarily only approximate reality. However, if one is prepared to settle for less than complete understanding, much can be learned

[2] Robert Redfield, "Relations of Anthropology to the Social Sciences and to the Humanities," in Sol Tax, ed., *Anthropology Today* (Chicago: University of Chicago Press, 1962), p. 458.

7

through observation of small, manageable communities. There, one can trace out the complicated interaction which underlies social change.

That is the course this study followed. Two small villages in India were selected. We spent four exciting months in the winter of 1961–1962 living in these villages, observing the relationship of communication and development. (If the plural crops up often in the pages that follow, there is good reason for it. My mother and I worked as a team during the investigation.) To get the specific information we needed we devised questionnaires and "administered" them very informally. (The details of the study design and field work, along with sample questionnaires, are given in the Appendixes.) We also checked official records. Let us begin the report of what we found out by taking a close look at the two villages, "Kothuru" and "Pathuru." [3]

[3] The names of the villages used here are fictitious. "Pathuru" means "old village" in Telugu, the main language of the area in which we worked. "Kothuru" means "new village." These particular names were adopted because they symbolize the purpose of the study: to compare and contrast communication in a village which has embraced some new forms of development like industrialization and one which continues, in large part, to depend on old ways, including the barter system.

CHAPTER 2

THE SETTING

BEFORE describing the two villages which have been singled out for detailed investigation as well as — and more important — for comparison and contrast, I should first point out a limitation on the material.

The selection of a specific problem virtually forces an investigator to confine himself to some aspects of community life, however wide the scope of the problem may be. While communication processes, economic activities, and signs of change in various areas, including political structure and social behavior, command attention here, they are not all treated with the same stress or in equal depth. A set of hypotheses guided our whole effort. I would like to believe that whatever was necessary to test the specific hypotheses in the field — filling out of questionnaires, inspection of official records, observation — has been done. But we did not attempt to gather information on all facets of life in the two communities. If such matters as child rearing or puberty rites fail to be mentioned here, it is not necessarily because they escaped our notice but because we felt discussion of them was not important for our purposes, indeed might unduly cloud the issues in hand.

First Impressions

A brief introduction to the two villages by way of "first impressions" seems necessary before going into a more detailed description of each of them, because it was on the basis of such impressions that Pathuru and Kothuru were decided upon. Their selection followed a series of visits to scores of villages — all confined to the state of Andhra Pradesh in South India in order to ensure some essential comparability (both villages had to be in the same administrative setup) and to take advantage of the investigator's ability to speak all four of the languages used in this state.

Our choice of villages was governed by the single overriding hypothesis that communication patterns as well as economic development will differ as between the traditional village and the "developing" village. Therefore, the search was focused on finding an "industrializing" village and a fairly comparable "non-industrializing" or "traditional rural" village. We eventually found Kothuru and, later, Pathuru which fitted our requirements and were also comparable in population. Whatever other differences there were between the two villages were left for later investigation.

As we rode into Kothuru by bus, we saw a row of neatly laid-out barrack-type buildings along the road just on the outskirts of the village. This, we were told, was the "Harijan colony," a new housing development for the "untouchable" castes which had formerly lived in dilapidated little huts on the edge of the village and close to the canal running through the village, making it necessary for them to huddle together in a few huts during the rainy season when the canal overflowed its banks. Between the new housing colony and the village proper was another neat group of buildings, separated by small compounds that surrounded each. These, we were told, housed the "Block Development Officers." A small group of government officials were in residence there.

Immediately after this we passed a large thatched "shed" (or what looked like a shed) and we were told it was the school building; then a large sign came into view. It read: "Tile Production-Cum-Training Center." Within a minute the bus stopped and we were in the village. Along with the other passengers, we got out and began to walk around the village. The "junction" (four roads cross at the point where the bus stops) was humming with activity and a number of shops lined the main road. There was a fair-sized restaurant on one corner, a small teashop on the corner across the street; there was also a barber shop and several little kiosks selling soft drinks, cigarettes, and so on. A 200-yard walk brought us to a little cottage industry located in a small building where about fifteen young men were busy working on unfinished horns of buffalo, turning them into polished birds, snakes, and the like. We were told they sold these objects to a handicraft cooperative in the city. A little more walking brought us to a carpentry shop where fairly modern furniture was being made by another group of young men under the guidance of an instructor who spoke to us in Telugu broken by a stray English word here and there. Almost directly across the road was a busy rice mill with two trucks standing by to pick up huge bags of processed rice carried on their backs by a stream of men. There were some women walking in and out of the mill, obviously workers.

We had seen enough. We checked the population with the village head who could only give us an approximate figure (about 2500, he said). We exchanged pleasantries with him and strolled about until it was time to catch the bus to return to the city. Throughout these hours in Kothuru, we were conscious of the fact that this was a busy community and few had the time (or the inclination) to look at us or wonder who these strangers were, not even when we went into the restaurant for a cup of coffee. The curiosity was perhaps there, but it was too mild to be noticeable. The residential part of the village was extremely quiet; most of the adults were away working in the fields surrounding the village, while the children were probably in school. We did not have enough time to see much else.

When we entered Pathuru, the reception was quite different. It was easy to sense immediately that many eyes were focused on us,

11

inquiries already being made in audible whispers about our identity and our business in their village. We were escorted around the village and constantly followed by many children and several older men (the women peered at us from behind doors). The principal market was right in the middle of the village, but it was more of an enclosed quadrangle than "main street"; houses too were clumped together and fields stretched in all directions from the village. The shops in the main *bazaar* (shopping area) were smaller than in Kothuru and not as well stocked. There was no restaurant, only one little teashop. There was no industry that we could see, but a number of artisans were working diligently at pottery, smithcraft, carpentry, and house-building. All of these were either individual enterprises or family "businesses" which, we found, were functioning to meet local demand only. Most of the houses were neat and well built and tiled. All the tile was locally made, our "guides" told us proudly. But none was sold outside the village. The closest we came to any "industry" was a small rice mill which, however, confined its milling to local produce for home consumption.

We went into the richest landlord's house, which was well insulated from the rest of the village. There was an old Vauxhall in the garage which had served the landlord well despite the condition of the *kutcha* (unpaved, and almost unintended) road that connects the village to the nearest town and highway five miles away. He lived in luxury — six months in the city, where his children were being educated, and six months in the village. He was also the *patel* (the person who takes care of police functions) of the village. His estimate of the population was "about 2500."

We had our second village.

Since we had promised anonymity not only to the village heads, but also to individual respondents (and this promise, we found, was greatly appreciated and unquestioningly accepted), we decided, as noted in Chapter 1, to call the two villages Kothuru and Pathuru, "new village" and "old village."

Our picture of the communities evolved gradually over the period of about two months that we spent in each of the villages. During this time we lived in the villages, in each of which we were provided with adequate accommodations. The first few days were spent in casual conversations and in achieving acceptance. This, we found, was extremely easy, especially because mother and son were together and they were living "just like any of us." Often we entertained some of our friends who would "drop in for a visit" or were invited to eat with them. This helped us become members of the "family" and yet remain fairly detached observers of a fascinating scene.

The "New Village": Kothuru

With his glasses perched precariously on the bridge of his nose, the *karanam* of Kothuru sits on the floor behind his little desk on which rests a massive book. He is entering some figures in the rows and columns into which each of the pages of the book is divided. But he is unable to continue his work for long, because the *karanam*, his desk, and his book are all on the open veranda of his house and the street which runs directly in front of his house ends at this low veranda. Any visitor wishing to talk to the *karanam* has merely to move directly from the street to the veranda and sit — all in one movement. If the *karanam* did not want to be disturbed, he could sit inside the house. But he does not mind being disturbed at all. He welcomes it. How else can he exchange information with the many friends he has in the village?

As *karanam*, his traditional job in the village is to keep account of agricultural transactions, land boundaries, and the like. It is a hereditary post. Much of the power has gone, thanks to the changes that have taken place since national independence, but influence is another thing. The *karanam* of Kothuru, whom we shall call Satyam, has less work as well as less power than earlier *karanams*. But he owns a fair amount of land and is content with the income he gets from it. He is sending one of his sons to college. He does not know whether his son will become *karanam* after him; he does not worry about it, for he has seen rapid changes in his own lifetime, and adapted to them willingly and graciously. If he ever looks upon his status in the community as a power position, one setting him apart from the general run of men, it does not show. He is gay, witty, extremely sociable, and rarely alone on the veranda. There are always friends dropping in on him, seeking his advice, passing on information, and exchanging notes. Seldom does the conversation become gossip, for Satyam will not stand for that kind of talk. Useful information, constructive criticism, or alternative suggestions, yes, but meaningless gossip, no. He can admonish with a parable or a hearty joke the unfortunate individual who unwittingly slips into gossip. But with all the information and all the influence that he so obviously has, he is not seeking any material or political benefits for himself. He is content with his social position. He is envious of neither the wealth of the richest man in the village nor the popularity of a man who was campaigning for political office at the time of our visit. In fact, it was Satyam who encouraged the political candidate to stand for election to the state assembly and took some of the latter's work (he was the *munsif* — the traditional judicial head of the village) on his own shoulders during the campaign. Satyam is well informed and can talk fluently on both economics and politics, but his real forte is philosophy.

In this single individual of the village, Kothuru's whole adaptation to change may very well be seen in crystallized form: the division of responsibilities in the social, economic, and political spheres; the acceptance of inevitable change with grace and forbearance; the gradual amalgamation of the new and the old; the strength and confidence with which an unknown future is faced, neither fear nor unrealistic hopes dimming reality; and the benign paternalistic attitude with which the younger generation and its "new-fangled ways" are tolerated because, in a changing world, "how can one expect not to change?"

Kothuru has not only heard of changes, but has seen them, and, at its own pace, is assimilating them. Fourteen miles from Kothuru is the busy seaport town of Visakhapatnam, which also happens to be the seat of the state university. Most of the changes brought into Kothuru today probably flow from there, for quite a few of Kothuru's residents have visited the city at least once, and a fair number of people come to Kothuru from Visakhapatnam, either on business or to visit relatives they left behind when they migrated to the city in search of jobs.

But, while all kinds of information come through these channels today, most of those who remember Kothuru's immediate history cite the war (World War II) as the starting point of the village's economic development. It was at that time, they say, that an army unit was stationed about ten miles from the village. The commandant of the unit visited Kothuru one day and suggested to the farmers in the village that he buy all the vegetables and the milk that they could provide. The offer was tempting and the few bigger farmers decided to take advantage of it. They had enough land to use part of it for cash crops while retaining their traditional pattern of cultivation on the rest, by which they produced both for their own consumption and for payment in kind to those who worked for them. It was not unpredictable that Kothuru would soon develop a money economy and would seek new investments. In this too the initiative was taken by the handful of rich landlords and farmers who had originally signed contracts with the army commandant.

As far as Kothuru's "historians" can remember, the first industry to be started was a rice mill. Others soon followed. The buying and selling that was involved, the recruitment of labor, the payment of wages to those removed from the land, the importing of skilled mechanics from the city, the necessity to attract more business from surrounding villages to keep the mills working at full capacity, and, today, the new uses that are being found for the extra money in peoples' pockets (the rich and the poor) — all have led to Kothuru's almost total metamorphosis economically. This has, no doubt, led to changes in social customs and in political patterns, but a great deal of the traditional way of life still remains. It is hard to tell, as Kothuru has adapted itself, how much is really old and imbedded, how much is new and revolutionary, and where the synthesis begins and ends. A more detailed consideration of the economic, social, and political structure of the village should give us some clues.

Economic Activity. While the original agreement with the army commandant led to a change in the pattern of cultivation and later to reinvestment in small industry, Kothuru remains a largely agricultural community like the rest of rural India. However, a money economy has almost completely replaced the traditional barter system. Even the handful of *palerus* (full-time servants of landlords who attach themselves and their families to the landlord completely and cannot seek even part-time employment elsewhere) left in the village now receive cash in addition to payments in kind, especially grain and housing. Instead of furnishing such goods as clothing and tobacco himself, the landlord finds it more convenient to give the *paleru* money to buy them. The one *paleru* whom we interviewed was being paid Rs. 0.40 (about 8 cents) a day. The rest of the agricultural laborers average Rs. 1.25 (about 25 cents) for a full day's work. During certain times of the year (harvesting, for example) when the urgency of the operation increases the demand for labor, the payment may go up to Rs. 2.00 (about 40 cents). The law of supply and demand has entered Kothuru's agricultural arena. There is as yet no labor union of any kind.

The migration of a large number of able-bodied workers to the city has introduced competition among the bigger farmers to secure the services of agricultural laborers and also to get the most out of them in the field. We interviewed one farmer while he was actively supervising a group of ten workers. They were permitted only an occasional glance in our direction. "They get paid well by me. Why shouldn't they work well, then?" the farmer said. He sees to it that they do, but in a polite tone. He knows he cannot be overbearing, for, unlike the *paleru*, his laborers can move whenever they want to, either to another farmer or to another occupation.

The choices for workers are several. There is industry; there is quarrying; there is transportation; and if all else fails there is the city, although most people still prefer to live and work in the village in which "we were born, our parents were born, and their parents before them." This attitude, which inhibits "mobility," is present to a great degree. However, there have been a large number (250 was the figure mentioned to us by several respondents) who have moved from the village in search of higher wages or better work. To what extent traditional attachment to village was broken down by economic *necessity* or forgotten because of economic *opportunity*, as

16

conveyed to the villagers by communicators of one kind or another, is hard to tell. But in Kothuru, one feels, each individual — the basically traditional person as well as the nontraditional — has chosen a path according to his own inclination. Kothuru's residents are adapting themselves to the changing patterns remarkably well and living in harmony.

It should be mentioned that most of those who have migrated to the city come back to the village at frequent intervals — not merely for a short visit, but for lengthy residence. Six months' work in the harbor and the shipyard at Visakhapatnam and six months back in the village helping on the family farm and living with the wife and children whom he had left behind is not an uncommon pattern of life for a young man of Kothuru. One young man, in his own way, summarized this life as close to "having one's cake and eating it too." He admitted, however, that if enough work were available in the village, he would rather stay there. He pointed out too that there were others who "liked the city ways" and did not want to come back to the village. Most of them did not have land in the village, or had quarreled with their families and taken cash for their share of the family land. As an economic asset, land still plays an important role in Kothuru. Therefore, despite the transition to nonagricultural occupations, the small landowner continues to call himself a cultivator even if most of his income comes from work away from his farm. This is reflected in the census data.

Out of a working population of 1234 (total population: 2992), 508 told the 1961 census enumerator that they were "cultivators"; the village clerk, who keeps a very close eye on the occupational pattern of the village, put the figure for industrial workers at 619. This would leave only 107 to fill all the other occupational categories. The official census, as a matter of fact, listed 337 as engaged in agricultural labor and 44 in household industry (artisans), these two groups alone amounting to more than triple the 107 apparently available! The explanation lies in the fact that a large percentage of those working as industrial laborers called themselves cultivators because they had a "small piece" of land; this land did not take much work and the little that it did take was being done by other members of the family.

It is our contention, then, that there are more people working in nonagricultural activities in Kothuru than the census shows. Enumerators are handicapped by their method as well as by the attitude of the villagers: pride of ownership of land or fear of tax on income.

It must be stressed, however, that agriculture does command the major amount of attention in Kothuru. It should also be noted that agriculture has taken on a new look. Processing of crops (especially paddy) has become an industry; farming is no longer merely for local consumption in a subsistence economy — the produce is sold in the market and necessities are bought with the money. An agricultural laborer is paid in money and he may buy with this money the same grain that he helped produce. The clear third step between producer and consumer has been taken, involving the middleman, in fact several middlemen — the specialized processor, the carrier, and the seller. Some kinds of agricultural produce, mainly rice, are exported; other kinds, mainly pulses and condiments, are imported. This has necessarily meant a proliferation of allied activities, such as shops, transport facilities, and some advertising, all leading up to a more modern economic and social community life which, by its very nature, also augments the flow of information.

The residents of Kothuru talk about prices of agricultural produce in terms of money and not in terms of a day's work or the equivalent in some other produce (e.g., one pound of rice as being equivalent to two pounds of maize — the situation in a subsistence economy working under the barter system, as we shall see in the case of Pathuru). They keep track of prices and seek information both as consumers and as producers; they will buy where the price is lowest and sell where it is highest because they have given up the family-to-family contract system which binds the traditional economy. The money economy that has transformed agricultural practices has also introduced new information into the individual's frame of reference: his frequent visits to shops have exposed him to the many things available there. He asks questions and gets the answers — information which he might never have obtained if agricultural practices had not changed.

This change is reflected in the number of people who are employed or act as independent entrepreneurs in ancillary activities, especially transport. Even if we take the census figures — which are probably too low — for those working in "transport, storage, and communications," the number is 99, a fairly high figure for a village in India. I have tried to indicate the process which led to the development of these ancillary occupations to show that the line between agriculture and industry is a difficult one to draw, especially in a rural economy such as Kothuru's. Any changes that do take place in the economic structure have to take place through agriculture, unless a specific village happens to be blessed with especially important mineral or other resources — in which case, the chances are that they have already been tapped and the village industrialized. Kothuru's case is more typical and, in the context of Indian economic development, more meaningful.

Industry in Kothuru grew out of agriculture, but has found new paths of its own. The original entrepreneurs were the rich landlords. The money they had acquired from cash crops as well as from the rice mills had to be invested somewhere. The fine new houses they built for themselves (one of them is especially "modern" in its design) are one sign of prosperity, but more significant for the village are the new activities they have branched into. These include one in which there is direct contact with the city — they have become contractors to supply sand and stone to urban entrepreneurs; they have also submitted bids for contracts to build roads even in areas fairly distant from Kothuru. One such man is the village *munsif* who obtained the contract to build a road six miles from the village. His success had repercussions in the village, in greater demands for labor, for trucks, and for raw materials, including stone which comes from quarries surrounding the village, untouched until recently.

The entrepreneural spirit which developed within Kothuru and strengthened its economy did not take long to spread to the nonelite, who found themselves not only richer economically but also more knowledgeable in the ways of the outside world. Their con-

19

tacts with the immediate surroundings (up to and including the city fourteen miles away) were expanding; at the same time their desire to improve themselves was increasing. Smaller entrepreneurs with less spectacular enterprises slowly entered the economic arena. These included the unemployed, or underemployed, farmer who opened a shop to sell *beedies* (an indigenous brand of cigar) and imported cigarettes, soft drinks, tea, and coffee powder. He had realized, on his own visits to the city, that as the villagers acquired new tastes and could afford to satisfy them, there would be a demand for such "luxuries" within the village itself. The next step, making soft drinks and bottling them, was not far off. It has already been taken in Kothuru by a widow with two growing children to feed.

As contacts with the outside world increased and more information flowed into Kothuru as well as out of Kothuru, entrepreneurs no longer were confined to the village. They began to come from outside, drawn by information received from Kothuru, just as residents of Kothuru went out to seek jobs on the strength of information received from the outside. The restaurant in Kothuru is operated by a man who does not talk the local language (Telugu); he came from a city where he had a smaller restaurant. His place of birth was in the state of Kerala, over 600 miles away. The restaurant in Kothuru, located in a two-storied building (the owner and his family live upstairs) at the crossroads, is very successful. The barber of the village opened a shop on the main road: he no longer goes to his customers; they come to him. The traditional custom of each member of the barber caste being attached to a number of families (and paid in kind) disappeared soon after the advent of a money economy.

News traveling from Kothuru has brought to the village the best educated man in the village today, a Vaisya (businessman caste) with a Bachelor of Commerce degree all the way from Vijayanagaram, a major metropolis in the state of Andhra Pradesh, where he had worked for a year as lecturer in commerce, but found he was still a businessman at heart. Today, he runs a fairly large rice mill in Kothuru and also undertakes the processing of groundnut (peanut) oil. In one year, he built up a fairly large operation, with the help of a local *pantulu* (a member of the Brahmin caste is frequently referred to by this title of respect, whatever his name), whose full-time occupation now is to get in touch with producers and buyers. In other words, the "middleman–public relations" job has been taken in Kothuru by a Brahmin to help a "foreign" Vaisya and help himself too in the process!

Many more examples of communication flow and of economic enterprise can be given for Kothuru, but the aim here is not to paint a complete canvas but only to indicate the broad signs of progress. The discussion so far has deliberately been confined to the "private sector" to show the potential of individual entrepreneurs. In addition chronological order has been observed. For government action in Kothuru came later, and whatever industrial or broad economic help the village received from the government was made available *after* some private development had already taken place.

Government assistance came mainly through the establishment of "production-cum-training" centers in tile manufacture, carpentry, and handicrafts, especially for the untouchable castes, the Harijans. There was a statewide village improvement scheme, under which "Block Development Officers" were to be put in charge of a number of villages (forty-three in Kothuru's Block) and were to be assisted by a staff of about six "extension officers," including an "extension officer — industry." This assistance came to Kothuru only in 1957. Contiguous with the village but at some distance from the heart of it is the Block Development Office and the residences of the small group of government officials. Although they are expected to visit and stay overnight, at least periodically, in all of the other villages around Kothuru which fall within the Block's jurisdiction, no one actually stays overnight. These officials would rather save all that effort for the weekends which they can spend in Visakhapatnam. Therefore Kothuru sees a great deal of them. This does not necessarily mean that village residents interact with them in any intimate way, but some exposure to city-bred people is constant in Kothuru.

Direct and intimate contact between government official and villager is restricted, so far as we could observe, to two of the extension officers, who by their charm and patience have encouraged villagers of all socioeconomic levels to stop them on the street and take their questions to them. The rest of the government personnel keep their distance except when the course of their duties makes contact inevitable. When this happens, the business in hand is usually quickly dealt with and the contact breaks. Since no effort is made by these government officials to be genial and friendly, the villagers do not dare "disturb" them, for, after all, even the petty government official is a "big man" in the eyes of the average villager. However, in Kothuru, it is not fear that keeps the villager away from the government worker; it is indifference mixed with traditional "respect" for the wealthy and the knowledgeable. The days when the people of Kothuru feared the government official are gone. Today, no official can ask a villager to run an errand for him — unless friendly relations have already been established.

The "extension officer — industry," whom we interviewed, attested to Kothuru's rapid development "in all respects" and added that the people had more amenities than before and were "craving for more." They were following new methods of production through the use of improved implements (electric pumps to water fields, iron-reinforced plows replacing the wooden) and marketing methods (use of trucks for heavy materials and cycles to take milk to the city — "all the milk goes to the city to be sold and we have no milk in the village!"). Kothuru had taken full advantage of the demand for its agricultural products, whether in the city or the surrounding villages or in the village itself, he added. He also put in a word for the government's two "major" projects in the area: tile manufacture and carpentry, for which too, he said, the demand had risen. In our interviews with workers in the factories (which also double as training centers) and from discreet inquiries elsewhere, we found that this was not entirely accurate. In fact, huge stocks of unsold tiles had prompted us to ask questions. Both the quality and the price, we were told, went against this product. Even Kothuru residents bought their tile elsewhere.

In the field of economic development, in other words, the government agencies have been able to do very little in Kothuru — *directly*. Indirectly, the fact that there are some well-informed (if not always very friendly or articulate) officials among the staff in residence has aided the villagers in obtaining information on the many things they are interested in. But it would not be proper for the government to take any credit for Kothuru's development in the economic field if the claim is based on the tile factory and the carpentry shop. These will not figure at all in any statistical estimate of Kothuru's economy, one can be fairly certain. Even the Harijan trainees in these two places are recruited with some difficulty. They can make a better living bootlegging. Kothuru is now officially dry; unofficially, however, "almost everyone drinks," we were told by an overwhelming majority of our respondents, including government officials as well as traditional leaders. One of them put it rather dramatically: Kothuru, he said, is an exceptionally "good" village in the area; only 95 per cent drink — "and this includes women and children." Most of the illicit brewing of the local drink (toddy) is done by Harijan families. With Kothuru's prosperity, they have a ready market. Since the men can no longer go to a shop and drink, they buy the bottles surreptitiously (and often not so surreptitiously, because it is no secret) and keep them at home, where the women and children have also begun to appreciate the beverage which, before prohibition, was supposedly a man's drink.

The Panchayat (the present unit of self-government in the village which, after 1959, was closely tied to the Block Development scheme under a state-wide reorganization of rural administration) might very well tap the liquor source for revenue to the benefit of the community as a whole, but it cannot, because prohibition is state policy. The present income of the Kothuru Panchayat is Rs. 4000 (about $800), according to the office clerk.

Much more can be said about Kothuru's economic development, and especially about the consciousness of economic change in the village, the resulting changes in speed of life, level of information, saving and investment, and so on, but these and other aspects will be taken up later in directly contrasting the two villages. At this point, some of the social and political patterns in Kothuru will be briefly touched upon to fill in the rest of the background necessary for a broad understanding of the community.

Social Structure. Like most Indian villages, Kothuru is a predominantly Hindu community and is conscious of caste differences. The few Muslims and Christians in the village are also conscious of their differences. While the "castes," among whom we can, for practical purposes, include the Muslims and the Christians, are all endogamous, they are not isolated into watertight compartments — not even the Harijans. But if one is looking for specific differences between the castes, their hierarchical order in the society, their rituals, customs, and taboos, there is no doubt that many can be found and described.

Our interest, however, stops at inquiring into how the differences among them affect either communication or economic development or both. Besides caste, we also have to consider other socioeconomic factors (e.g., the elite-mass gap) which affect our specific problem.

Mention has already been made of the Harijan colony of Kothuru. This was constructed as part of the government's program of "Harijan uplift," under which housing, sanitation, education, and vocational training are all provided for the hitherto "backward classes" of India. To this extent the Harijans are now a "favored" class, and they are taking advantage of the benefits offered. Especially heartening in Kothuru is the response the Harijans have made to educational facilities. Harijan children who until a few years ago could not sit with "caste Hindus" in classrooms, today are students in Kothuru's two schools, like any other children, and parents of "caste Hindu" children do not complain about the "pollution." Nor, for that matter, does the "Brahmin" restaurant keeper consider the Harijan's money any less legitimate than that of his other customers'. Harijans are also working side by side with members of other castes in industrial centers, in training centers, and in the fields; they are sitting next to other caste members in buses and trains and lorries (a cheap and popular mode of travel in Kothuru's expanding transport business — truck drivers take passengers if their vehicles are not loaded to the brim with material). Caste differences have, therefore, not substantially affected either economic development or communication in Kothuru.

In religious ceremonies, which have decreased, marriages, and group eating on festive occasions, caste continues to play a major

24

role in rural India. This is also true of Kothuru. However, since most of the interpersonal relationships in which meaningful information is exchanged take place outside the home (in work centers, shops, roadside meetings, and the like), class and caste differences do not significantly affect the scope for effective communication between people of different social groupings — so long as contacts outside the home take place. In Kothuru they do.

Caste differentiation in occupation has begun to break down in Kothuru at a very fast pace. Economic opportunity has imperceptibly brought about social change and social change itself has contributed to further economic development. The Harijan skilled laborer commands respect from the Vaisya trainee in Kothuru. If caste differences had stayed rigid, the skilled mechanic from the city could not have been imported into the village.

Over 50 per cent of our respondents in Kothuru were working in jobs other than what they were "meant for" under the caste-occupation rules of ritualized Hinduism. The Kothuru priest's remarks in this connection were edifying. Kothuru's residents, he said, no longer are tied to ritual. They do not go to the temple mechanically, except on some big festival day. "They are thinking more of the philosophy of their religion." He may have been exaggerating to some extent, considering Kothuru's large number of illiterates and those incapable of thinking in the abstract. The priest himself no longer stays in the temple; he works for a living in other vocations — farming and astrology. He continues to be a part-time priest, going to homes to perform private rituals for individual families.

Kothuru's "development" and change in the social structure can also be seen in the fact that fewer women work in the fields or at other occupations. They have become "housewives." According to the local midwife, women are more anxious than men to send their children to school, to send their boys to the city to find jobs, and to practice family planning. Knowledge of public affairs among them, however, is still extremely limited; only their knowledge of economic opportunities and the importance of education and of restricting families so as to reduce the pressure on land has increased. The midwife was also pleased at the women's response to sanitation drives, health clinics, child-care demonstrations, and the like, which have been arranged by government agencies or private social work organizations. The kind of information in which the women are interested is vastly different from that which attracts the attention of the men, but as complementary units the men and women of Kothuru seem to have divided their labors well.

This is especially true in the upper echelons, but since the vast disparities in socioeconomic levels are slowly being lessened, the trend is seen in the lower brackets too. This bridging of the elite-mass gap is most evident in its manifestations in social relationships between men. The Panchayat president, who also happens to be the richest landlord and contractor of Kothuru, is stopped often on the road by other villagers, rich and poor; so is the friendly *karanam* who has already been mentioned. The *munsif* is perhaps the best example of Kothuru's bridging of the gap. He is not only approached, but goes out of his way to greet and talk to other villagers, each of whom he knows personally. To say that the *munsif* does this because he is running for office in the state assembly and needs votes would be to disregard completely his personality, which is warm, friendly, philosophic, and even crusading. It may be closer to the truth to say that he was urged to run for office by the Congress party because of his popularity, not only in Kothuru, but also in some of the surrounding villages in the constituency. We talked to him at great length and it was not difficult to see why he was popular. He respects every human being, high or low. He himself had worked as a laborer in Burma many years ago and knew what it was to be low in the socioeconomic hierarchy. His influence in the village is unmistakable.

While government officials and other city-bred people either resident in Kothuru or visiting on business have no doubt influenced the thinking and the attitudes of the villagers, the role of the "intermediaries" (the younger educated men) cannot be ignored in the total picture of social change in Kothuru. They are far closer to the villagers than the visitors; their contacts are more frequent and more effective. Added to this is the villagers' direct exposure to the city in their own travels and their own reading of the "morals" in the movies which they seem to see so often. The cumulative effect of the various kinds of exposure (direct and indirect) is apparent in Kothuru.

Political Structure. Interest in politics in Kothuru is low. Even local politics do not seem to arouse much enthusiasm. There are no aggressively divided factions. To a stranger visiting Kothuru for the first time and spending some time in the village, the obvious quiet and serene indifference to people may be almost unnerving. He has not expected this kind of welcome in rural India; he is not prepared to be ignored as in a city.

A political meeting was held in Kothuru while we were there. A jeep drove in with a leader of the Congress party who was to address a meeting in the larger school building (the primary school has a large, well-built hall, while the high school is in a temporary thatched shed). We were invited by the *munsif* for "tea and biscuits" with the speaker before the meeting. As we walked out of the little room in which the small group of those specially invited had met, a few minutes before the scheduled time for the meeting, and made our way through the village to the school building at the other end of the village, few heads turned to see who the VIP was, few followed the small procession of "dignitaries" around the speaker. When we entered the school hall, however, we saw about forty people already squatted on the floor and ready to listen to the visitor. Throughout the meeting, it was hard to refrain from wondering how forty people had been collected when no one on the main road seemed to be interested in the visitor or the meeting. We found later that Youth League volunteers had literally rounded up some stray villagers by mild threat and entreaty. The *munsif's* name brought most of the "audience" — not the visitor's.

The role of the Youth League is interesting. It is not a political organization. Its main interest is drama; the *munsif* is himself a good writer and actor. Hence the volunteers' interest in the meeting and in the *munsif's* candidacy for the state assembly. When he goes campaigning in the surrounding villages, he gets most of his entourage from among the ranks of the Youth League, which has twenty members who pay Rs. 2.00 (about 40 cents) for membership. Each gets a baton to set him off from the others in village meetings. Almost to a man, the members are young and educated, and are avid readers of newspapers and magazines. They are all for the Congress party, and with that statement, their interest in politics seems to end. "The whole village is for Congress," one of our Youth League respondents said, "and no other candidate has a chance. Any other candidate has to come from outside the village. He will be allowed to talk and go from door to door to canvass. He may even put up some posters. But I know he will get no votes."

Kothuru's adult population is not even interested in local politics. Elections to the village Panchayat do not stir them, for there are no factions. Candidates have to be found to take their positions on the Panchayat Committee. These are usually respected members of the community, from the landlord to the Harijan leader, who happens to be an educated farmer, modest, hard-working, articulate without being bombastic, and intelligent. He was the obvious choice for the Harijans, who, under the Panchayat Act, are entitled to at least one representative.

However, if decisions taken by the Panchayat in cooperation with the Block Development Office (and this cooperation is very close) are not palatable to the villagers, they are outspoken. The criticism is usually directed toward the "B.D.O." (Block Development Officer) and not the Panchayat. The villagers know that many government decisions made at state headquarters are implemented in the village with no reference to village requirements. An expenditure of Rs. 3000 (about $600) on two public lavatories, one respondent told us, was a sheer waste of "our money," because "we will never use the lavatories. Why couldn't they use the money on something we need?" The same man will express himself in similar terms to some of the Panchayat members. They will tell him that it was really government money which the B.D.O. was asked to spend on lavatories and that he had no choice either. There the matter will rest, the incident forgotten — also the lavatories.

The Kothuru resident is conscious of the government, especially since the B.D.O. is right in his backyard, but he is not dependent on it. Hence, he can make use of the good and forget the bad. He uses the government's health center to its full capacity, goes to the "agri-

28

cultural extension officer" for fertilizer, but if the government, for one reason or another, is unable to help him, he can either help himself or turn to another activity. If one of the government officers is a "nice man," he will talk to him; otherwise, he will stay out of his way.

Through the Block they have heard of some "plan" but are not clear about where the five-year plans originate and why.[1] Their horizons have widened enough to encompass "Andhra" and vaguely "India" but at the more conscious level, it is "Kothuru" and "Visakhapatnam," "Panchayat" and "Block," which have real meaning for them.

The political or economic structure beyond what they can see, feel, and directly hear is unintelligible to most of Kothuru's residents except the few who are educated, informed, traveled, or in positions of some responsibility. Otherwise, most of Kothuru's residents are so bound up in their own affairs (especially economic betterment) that they leave politics for those who like it.

Communication Patterns. In this description of Kothuru, the patterns of communication have deliberately been relegated to the end, for communication, as defined here, can only be clearly seen within the cultural context of a community. That context should now be at least reasonably clear. Equally clear, however, is the fact that communication's own role in the complicated process of Kothuru's development and present state of mind is imbedded inextricably in the process itself, just as economic development, social change, and political patterns are interwoven. Certain aspects of communication in Kothuru have already been described as they affected or were affected by the changes that have taken place: the army commandant's request for vegetables and milk, the presence of sources of information in the village in the form of friendly government officials as well as visiting dignitaries, although the officials may be sought out and the dignitaries virtually ignored by most of the villagers.

It is clear also that it is almost impossible to chart the flow of any

---

[1] India's development programs are centralized, for the most part, in a series of five-year plans. Very often this whole effort, as well as any specific part of it, is referred to simply as the "plan" or "planning."

given item of news and say with any amount of confidence that between source and terminant the particular news item went through such and such steps. In the highly diffused pattern of Kothuru's social intercourse it is perhaps even impossible to tell source from terminant at any given point in time.

The villager's memory about the source of news, unless he gets it directly from one of the media, seems to be extremely poor in Kothuru. A series of questions concerning this in the information level part of our general questionnaire worked, we found, only at the "first step" if that step happened to be one of the media. Otherwise, a typical answer was "Oh, somebody told me." Only in a very few cases did respondents name a specific source. In these cases, the source was always the same — a single other person, a man who "reads the newspaper and is very intelligent." The number of acquaintances of such respondents, we found, was exceptional for Kothuru. These respondents seemed to be extremely withdrawn and interacted only with one or two others. Only in such cases was it possible to check the source of news, and these were exceptions which proved the rule: that communication in Kothuru is highly dynamic, traveling through the maze of interpersonal relationships which make up the total community. Communication literally takes the form of the society itself.

The picture of Kothuru's communication pattern is certainly not complete without consideration of its media participation. Even in our sample, which consisted of a far greater proportion of elite than the proportion in the total population, less than 50 per cent cited the newspaper as their source of news for one of a series of six items in our information test, and 100 per cent acknowledged oral communication as a source. The media must take a back seat in Kothuru, at least for the present.

However, it must also be pointed out that within the national pattern of media consumption (eleven newspapers per 1000 population), Kothuru presents not too bad a picture. Twenty-four copies of newspapers are bought in the village in addition to ten subscriptions directly delivered by mail. Six of these copies are delivered to the Block Development Officer and his staff who live slightly separate from the village and whose newspapers are therefore presumably not shared except by their own families, but twenty-eight copies are shared in Kothuru. From our interviews with newspaper subscribers and with the librarian, we estimated that the average number of readers for each of these 28 copies was seven.

Radio was a poor second to newspapers among the media. There are ten radio sets in Kothuru, including the Panchayat radio. The average number of listeners to news programs was five. As a source of news, then, radio came after oral communication and the newspaper.

Education is popular. In the two schools, there were a total of 315 boys and girls at the time we were in the village (an increase of 50 in one year) and the attendance was "excellent" according to the two teachers we interviewed, one each from the primary school and the high school. But both of them complained that the attendance of girls falls off after primary school, because "their mothers seem to need them at home."

We were also told that there was "enthusiasm" for adult education but no steps had been taken to fill this need.

From the postmaster we found that the amount of mail coming into the village had increased and the number of telegrams had gone up from 14 to 35 in two years.

While no exact records are kept of travel to and from Kothuru, the station master said it had increased by 30 to 40 per cent in the preceding three years. He knew of no foreigners who had visited Kothuru, but there were many businessmen from other states of the country who had stopped by. The bus driver whom we talked to also spoke of the significant increase in passengers and consequently of bus services to Kothuru. Even the dozen or so buses which connect Kothuru with Visakhapatnam and a few other towns do not seem to fill the need, and, as indicated above, trucks have been picking up "standing passengers" for a nominal charge.

The librarian of Kothuru, an extremely conscientious worker, gave us the figures on magazine and book reading. These had not shown any great increases during his tenure, but he thought the prospects were good, considering the fact that the library was still comparatively new (one and a half years old) and new books were coming. He said that twenty-four members of the library borrowed books with some regularity; most of them read novels. Of those who use the magazines and newspapers, 30 per cent, he said, were below the age of twenty, 50 per cent in the twenty to forty-five bracket, and 20 per cent were above forty-five. He put the average number of readers in the reading room at thirty-eight per day, as compared with twenty-six the previous year.

There is no movie house in Kothuru, but it was hard to come by a single adult who had not at one time or another seen a movie in one of the towns nearby. Most of them had gone to movies in Visakhapatnam. Over 70 per cent of our respondents were fairly regular moviegoers ("about once or twice a month"). This reflected not only their exposure to the movies, but also their travel habits. Over 50 per cent of our respondents had traveled beyond Visakhapatnam, some of them to North India, a distance of over 1000 miles.

Kothuru, in more senses than one, is on the move. In this process, it is exposing itself to all kinds of new experiences and new information. The information sources are many — both inside and outside the village. Contacts are many. Economic development is explained by most of the elite respondents in terms of "contact" with outsiders. Only two of our elite respondents specifically mentioned the media as one of the reasons for change in people's habits, whether in dress or eating or thinking.

Kothuru's preoccupation with economic development is reflected in its pace of life and in its information level. More people have heard of the increase in the price of *tamarind* (a kind of spice) and of life insurance than of Russia exploding the "big bomb" or of a high-level committee visiting the state to inquire into the sharing of waters between Andhra and two adjoining states. Most have not heard of the state chief minister either. It is obvious that they seek certain kinds of information; if certain other kinds of information come to them, they retain what falls in their frame of reference and forget the rest. Those high in information level are the elite and persons in some power positions. To the rest, "general news" is a luxury they cannot afford now. But they do have ways of getting the news they are interested in. Sources are usually readily available within the village. If not, they can obtain the information from the city.

The "Old Village": Pathuru

As one walks along the narrow street leading from the main *bazaar* to the northern section of the village of Pathuru, he passes the house of the local *karanam*. It is a big house, cemented and two-storied, with a large compound running around it. A small gate serves as an entrance to the house. If one dares go through it, he walks another 100 feet before coming to the main door of the house. This door is wide open, unlike the street entrance which is only slightly ajar during the day. Directly in front of the main door sits the *karanam*, on a long bench. In front of him is a large table and a heavy book in which he is entering some figures. On one side of the table is a chair; on the other side, about six feet away from him, is a large, low bench. It is a big hallway in which he sits. This, as well as the fact that he is all alone, somehow makes him look small, and yet he may give others the impression that he is big, because apparently he does not want to be disturbed. He is the "ruler" of rural Pathuru and this is his "castle." At least so he may think in his isolation. At the age of sixty, perhaps he hopes to be able to pass the rest of his life believing that he is the leader of the village, no matter what changes have been taking place outside his own four walls.

It is not difficult to find out that he is, in fact, unaware of the changes that have taken place in his "own people," or if he is aware of them, he is deliberately shutting himself away from them. After two meetings with him, it was apparent to us that of some changes, he is unaware; he is aware of others but refuses to acknowledge them. The lack of acknowledgment is, however, aggressive, and bitterness shows through.

"Is life in the village happy?" we asked him. "No," came the reply, sharp and clear. He added: "Life was better in the old days. People were contented. Now contentment is gone. And where there is no contentment, people cannot be happy. Everyone wants to become like the rich man. That is not possible, because they do not have the brains to think."

The *karanam* has not heard about any five-year plan, but knows a little about the Panchayat and the fact that the government "is doing something." He adds: "God knows what they are doing, but this much I know, they are making a mess!"

Questions on empathy brought an interesting response from the *karanam*. He had no difficulty putting himself in the position of the head of the village, although he is not the Panchayat president (today's village head). But when we asked him what he would do if he were the chief minister of the state, he replied: "You are asking me a silly question. It is like asking a fellow who does not know O, Na, Maha [the Sanskrit alphabet], to recite Sloka [a poem] number 248 and interpret it." After that rebuff, we did not go on to our third level to ask him if he could put himself in the shoes of India's prime minister.

The *karanam* of Pathuru symbolizes the tragedy of the village. By isolating himself from the "stupid masses" he learns nothing and he teaches nothing. Meanwhile, the changes that have been brought into the village have created confusion because no explanation of them has been made available. The *karanam* is certainly capable of understanding, but does not want to make the effort. With one or two exceptions, the rest of the traditional elite are more or less of the same temperament. Some of them are extremely well informed, but show no inclination to use this information for anything but their own advantage, and often not even that. They are contented with about 200 acres of land each and a palatial home in the middle of deprivation, ignorance, and discontent.

As "gatekeepers," they are doing an extremely effective job of keeping things of the modern world out and themselves in. Another big landlord in the village who also happens to be the police *patel*, with an even bigger house and a bigger compound than the *karanam*, closes both his doors and posts a watchman inside the outer door. When he visited us in our little one-room quarters, he had to walk through the village and this was big news. Apparently he had not walked through the village in years, only driven out of it in his Vauxhall on a road that skirts the village.

However, the people of Pathuru have seen buses come down the same road and turn into the village and pass through to another village five miles away. The brief stop that the bus began to make two years before our visit and all the events that have occurred since then, including visits from government officials in their first attempts at reorganizing the Panchayat and explaining to a few of the elite that the village was now part of the Block Development scheme, have opened new possibilities. But after the government officials left, the elite, if they listened to what was explained to them, never told the people what it was all about. So, an enterprising few, acting as "intermediaries," took upon themselves the job of finding out, led both by curiosity and a genuine desire to know what they could do.

We met a few of these young men and one or two older men who have been attempting to fill the gap left by the disinclination of the elite to provide information. Theirs is a difficult task, for they command neither the respect (not untinged with traditional fear) that the landlord does, nor the unquestioning faith that is placed in a "neutral" source such as a government official who, after all, is not in any village faction. However, this handful of men, with tenacity, are slowly gaining ground. It remains an uphill task, with the government officials sitting in the Block headquarters, five miles away and rarely condescending to drop in (for two years before we came, no government official had visited the village for any length of time, except the "village level worker" who was more concerned about selling his quota of small savings certificates — a sure way of losing friends and influencing none — than of inquiring into the villagers' needs), and the elite serenely enjoying their riches either by frequent visits to the city themselves or by sending their children to school and college in the city.

The city is twenty-five miles away — Hyderabad, the capital of Andhra Pradesh, and the seat of Osmania University, the world-famous Nizam, and Salar Jung Museum, noted for its rare collections of the most precious antiques and of documents. It is about two hours by bus if one takes the "cross-country service" which two enterprising entrepreneurs have provided for Pathuru and surrounding villages which are not connected by direct roads to the metropolis. A person who cycles five miles to Ibrahimpatnam can catch one

35

of many buses going to and from Hyderabad at frequent intervals. Keen competition between the two entrepreneurs has made the "cross-country service" very popular and a large number of Pathuru's residents have visited Hyderabad and seen movies there. They would like to go oftener, but cannot afford it, for Pathuru's economy has not developed from within. The landlords who have the money have invested it outside the village; the rest are subsisting on traditional occupations and on uneconomic land holdings, waiting for the day when things will get better, but not knowing how or from where the bounty is going to come. Meanwhile, they are an utterly discontented lot, "lost" amid the confusion of the clash between change and the rigid forces of tradition. An indefinable and unnerving potential for development can be felt, but what form eventual "progress" will take depends on what happens or what is done between now and that not-too-distant future. The appetites *have* been stirred but no ways to satisfy them shown.

Economic Activity. Pathuru's economic structure has changed very little in many years, despite political change brought about by India's independence and, especially, the end of the princely state that was Hyderabad. Most economic exchanges are still conducted under the barter system, although the value of money, as well as its use, is fully understood. Where almost the whole economy is agricultural and household-oriented in a self-sufficient community such as Pathuru, barter is a convenient system, especially since much of the pattern was set long ago and very little has happened since then to justify any major change. If a person needs money for some reason, say to visit the city, he can always sell his "wages" (in grain) to the local Vaisya businessman and ask for payment in money rather than an equivalent amount of some other necessity. Since visits to the city have increased and some new kinds of shops have come into the village where barter is not practiced, the use of currency is slowly increasing.

Most agricultural labor is, however, still paid in kind, unless for one reason or another the landlord decides to pay in cash. Usually, it is the landlord who decides. If he thinks he can do better by selling his particular crop in the city, he will pay wages in currency. The average payment for a day's work is Rs. 0.50 (10 cents). Except in very rare cases such as an unplanned synchronization of plowing or transplanting of paddy on all the lands, labor is fairly easily available and therefore the occasion to increase wages does not occur. Also, most landlords have their own "regulars" who would rather wait for work from them than go to another cultivator and incur the displeasure of their regular landlord. Under such conditions, little competition has developed, and therefore little increase in wages.

The landlords' view, however, is different. They want their children not only to be educated in the city, but to find jobs there. "There is no future for them in this village," is the most common remark of the rich landlords when questioned about their plans for their children. In other words, the landlords' expectations for economic development rest with the city; the mass do not look beyond the village. If economic development is to take place on a broad base, the mass have to be shown opportunities and these opportunities have to be shown in the village, not in some distant place. Both the elite and the government (the only other agency capable, under the circumstances, of taking on the mantle of entrepreneur or informant) have failed to show the mass in Pathuru any opportunity. The "intermediaries" have only barely started to become effective as informants.

In the absence of knowledge of any other activity, the typical resident of Pathuru clings to his little piece of land or his tools and continues to eke out a living doing as many odd jobs as he can find, but these are few. So he relies mainly on his original caste occupation and becomes a burden, both to his family and to himself. There is no possibility for specialization beyond what was set up under the caste-occupation system centuries ago. If he is born a Chakali (washerman), he still continues to call himself a Chakali, even if he works as a farm laborer, if and when he does work.

According to the census (there are no other figures available in the small Panchayat office of Pathuru, run by an eighteen-year-old clerk who is both inefficient and otherwise busy running a cycle shop), 1375 out of a total population of 2617 work. This is almost the entire adult population, including women. There are few housewives in Pathuru and these are confined to the rich homes. Every extra penny brought in by a member of the family can be used. "Education is for the children of rich parents. Poor people like us must work, and that includes our children."

Agriculture, in its most fundamental form of growing a crop, processing it at home, and eating it, occupies the largest proportion of Pathuru's population. "Household industry," the official name for artisans who provide for the other necessities of the village by well-digging, washing, forging, and pottery-making, encompasses almost the whole of the rest of the working population. Only recently, a canal being dug a few miles from the village has provided work for what is now called "bunding labor." The few shops take care of the remaining workers, including the Vaisyas, who, by birth, are businessmen and who, by proclaiming themselves such, exaggerate the census figures for "trade and commerce" to forty-three, although the few shops in the *bazaar* do very little business.

Entrepreneural spirit is little evident in Pathuru. It is confined to two Muslims who run a teashop and a cycle shop, and a Kapu (farming caste) who recently opened a grocery store. One Vaisya, also recently, opened a ready-to-wear clothing shop.

Social Structure. Religious and caste differences exist in Pathuru; to some extent they are relatively more pronounced than in Kothuru, but their effect in the area of communication is not as strong as it could be if the castes or the religious groups did not mix at all. In Pathuru, there is just one Christian family but there are thirty Muslim families, a fairly common phenomenon in Hyderabad's rural area, stemming from the fact that the princely state of the erstwhile Nizam was predominantly governed by Muslims although the large majority of the population was Hindu.

The interaction of these two groups has led to the strange mixture of languages in and around Hyderabad. In Pathuru, for example, the Telugu spoken by the Hindus has a large number of Urdu words, and the Urdu, spoken by the Muslims, likewise has taken in a large number of Telugu words. Almost the entire population is bilingual; hence any barrier to communication must be sought in other areas. For the interviewer, however, a knowledge of both these languages is almost essential, because otherwise he will be unable to get the full meaning of responses in either language. Also, speaking in Urdu brings ready responses from the Muslim respondents. Being the minority, they are more conscious of their differences, and they cherish their rich language. A stranger who greets them in Urdu and talks in Urdu is immediately treated as a friend.

While caste and religious differences do minimize certain kinds of contact in Pathuru — intermarriage, inter-dining, and so on — they do not affect others. In ordinary social intercourse in public places, few caste differences can be readily seen by a stranger, except in the case of the Harijan, who still maintains his distance from the caste Hindus for fear of offending them. He has every reason for doing this, because many caste Hindus have reacted very strongly against Harijan children being sent to the local school. Generations of Harijans have borne this type of discrimination in Indian villages even after the advent of Gandhi and his campaign against untouchability (resulting in several legislative measures to root out this practice) with resignation and humility. It is perhaps a significant indicator of the degree of Pathuru's adaptation to social change that it continues to draw a clear line between "caste Hindus" and "casteless Hindus" to whom Gandhi gave the name "Harijans," meaning "children of God."

But there are other indications too of Pathuru's inability to progress. Some of these have been mentioned in discussing its economic structure, especially the caste-occupation relationship. In the social structure, many of the same patterns show. Each subcaste (or a group of them) has its temple, but all are deserted. Two of the local priests, each of whom is nominally in charge of a temple, are earning a meager living on the small piece of land attached to the temple and adding to their incomes by dabbling in *ayurveda* (an Indian medical system which relies heavily on the use of herbs). One of the priests has recognized the gullibility of the villager in his insistence on being given an "injection," whatever the ailment may be (he has heard of the "immediate relief" an injection gives). So the "priest-doctor" gives injections without being qualified in any way to handle a surgical needle.

The most significant aspect of the social structure of Pathuru is perhaps its inability to bridge the elite-mass gap. The disparity between the rich and the poor shows up in the almost total lack of communication between the two, save only for the handful of "intermediaries" who have access to the one group because of their own socioeconomic status and to the other because of their political, social, or, in stray cases, plain humanitarian ambitions. These intermediaries are the most garrulous and active persons in Pathuru, as well as the best informed. To some extent, however, they are the instigators of factionalism. They are grouped on one side. The other faction is inactive, but powerful. The landlords and traditional leaders still hold the reins of power in Pathuru and the intermediaries are the young rebels. While the young rebels and their audience hold court in the *bazaar*, talking about the same things, over and over again, the big landlords are at home, impervious to all that is going on around them. So are most of the poorest and illiterate members of the community, to whom all this talk seems to be somehow unethical, for to think such thoughts about the "big men" does not come to them naturally, after years of serfdom.

So the Gaondlas (toddy tappers) are in their group of houses, the Kurumas (shepherds and weavers) in theirs, and the Komatis (businessmen) in theirs. But they are talking their own gossip in little groups. Quite apart from the village, but not too far from it, is the Harijan colony, a large group of pathetic-looking huts, in marked contrast to the tiled houses that most of the others seem to have built for themselves. This grouping sets the pattern for Pathuru's social structure, which, as is no doubt apparent, cannot be separated from the economic and political structure. Each impinges on the other and in Pathuru's case it becomes especially difficult to describe them as disparate activities or isolatable systems.

The women of Pathuru "live exactly the same lives" as they have always done, said one of our respondents, the midwife of the village. On family planning, there is neither talk nor action. "Long ago, somebody came into the village and told them about it. They have already forgotten about it, since there has been no continued propaganda. So no action, no talk — only children," she added. The attitude of women toward sending children to school has not changed either. "Is education going to feed us?" is their counter-question to suggestions or inquiries. Nor do they want to send their children to the city to work. They are afraid of what may happen to the children in the city. Few women have been exposed much to the city, although most of the men have frequently visited it.

The midwife of Pathuru, a trained social worker, has become a cynic. The odds are too great for her to cope with alone, and she has no help whatsoever. It was obvious that she had not started out a cynic, or she would not have embarked on a career which she knew would take her to backward villages. In the two years that she had been in residence in Pathuru, the village had shown no signs of change, she said, talking especially of the women. She pleaded for "more education" and she mentioned "propaganda." She may very well have been thinking of the need for "communication," as a means of bringing about needed change in the attitudes of women, who have such strong influence on how the next generation is going to turn out. Pathuru's social structure has shown little change. One has to look hard to find rays of light penetrating the hard mud walls. If one is trained to do so and puts in the effort, he can see a glimmer here and a glimmer there. But one can hardly expect a midwife, all on her own, to do much. It is up to Pathuru's men, and there are only a few stalwarts among them.

Political Structure. The stalwarts one can find operate mainly in the political arena, for they have limited economic power and limited social status. They have to gain positions of political power before they can influence the decisions made for a nominally democratic community by the firmly entrenched elite, who continue in the authoritarian way in which they were reared, despite the lip service they pay to the Panchayat system. They see no possibility of challenge because they have shut themselves off from the mass whom they consider "ignorant." The mass, however, are not as ignorant as the elite seem to think. Over the years, the young stalwarts have patiently sown seeds of discontent.

Pathuru today is acutely discontented. The last Panchayat election was proof of it, although most of the elite to whom we mentioned the event shrugged it off as reflecting one of the "factional" jealousies in the village. In one ward during the election, almost 100 per cent of the voters turned out, including an eighty-five-year-old woman who had to be brought to the polling booth on a stretcher. The rebel group lost by a hair's breadth, but they had gained the necessary confidence that their cause will eventually win. The leader of this cause is the Congress leader for the region who is also a fairly well-to-do farmer. In his latter capacity, he has access to the big landlords' homes and sits and talks with them as an equal. They do not discuss politics, however.

Pathuru's political interest stops at the local level. It is also hard to tell how much of all the talk that goes on in small groups is gossip and how much politics, because political activity has become personal, and extremely so. The vehemence with which the character of certain landlords and power holders is attacked by the rebels defeats its very purpose, for the average villager, who is generally apathetic, puts it down to personal rivalry. He has never been taught to think in terms of self-government or equality. These terms mean nothing to him. All he knows is that he is a lowly laborer working for the "big man" who has always taken care of him and his family. When he goes to the polling booth, he votes for the *patel* or for whomever his caste head tells him to vote. The caste head is himself a laborer working for the *patel*. Unless and until some economic "equality" has been achieved or the dependence of the landlord on his labor has been explained to the mass, it will be hard for the average villager to react any other way. Since the supply of labor is plentiful in Pathuru's closed economy, the worker has not had a chance to recognize his own importance; on the other hand, he recognizes the landlord's importance and automatically transfers it to the political field also. He does not have enough knowledge to understand the difference. For as long as he can remember, all power — social, economic, and political — has been in the "big man's" hands. The only division of labor he has ever known is the caste differentiation which extends to occupation, regardless of ability or aptitude.

Therefore, if a man is economically poor and socially low, he is necessarily politically impotent. That is why the few rebels are the "in-betweens" who are neither so high that they have power to guard nor so low that they do not think they have any right to seek it. They are a hardy lot, but they can do with some help. They cannot get very much from within the village; from the outside, there seem to be few possibilities. But as long as their energies last, there is hope that the average resident of Pathuru will become politically conscious.

Communication Patterns. Much of Pathuru's general communication pattern has already been indicated indirectly in describing its economic, social, and political structures. We have seen that communication flows almost entirely horizontally, except for a few intermediaries. Caste groupings (including the Muslims as a distinct group in the social structure), economic disparities, occupational limitations, all lead to the formation of almost distinct peer groups. Communication not only remains within the group, but invariably tends to be highly repetitive. Since little information that is new comes into the village, the old and trivial information is a perennial source from which to draw to fill the vacant evenings.

Several times during our stay in the village, we heard the five-year-old story of Pathuru's experience with the cholera epidemic. It was suspected that the disease was the direct result of *mantras* (religious chantings, very much akin to witchcraft, but not necessarily used for evil purposes) chanted by a small group of Chakalis (washerman caste) early one morning, when they were seen bathing on the banks of the narrow canal skirting the village. Of all people, the local midwife (the present incumbent's predecessor) had reported the chantings. In the transmission of the story, it was no doubt embellished. When cholera struck, the incident was recalled and the Chakalis beaten and exiled by the whole village. The leader of the Chakalis, in relating the story to us, said he had gone to the landlord, who had migrated to Hyderabad with his family during the epidemic, to seek his help. The landlord knew full well that the Chakalis were innocent; also that cholera does not come at the beck and call of a small group of *mantra*-chanters. But he would not intervene. Health units of the government later came and cleaned up the village and the epidemic subsided after taking its toll.

43

Five years later, the story was recalled in all detail and described over and over again, although the small group of exiled Chakalis had been back in the village for two years and their leader was a highly respected member of the community.

For the people of Pathuru, there are many incidents such as this one; all of them belong to the past and all of them concern the village — either the entire community or specific individuals, like the present vice-president of the Panchayat who had been sent to jail for six months some years before for stealing the *karanam*'s jewelry, and who, while we were there, was accused of having raped one of the women working for him on his fields. These are the stories which keep Pathuru talking after the small oil lamps have been put out soon after dark, for oil is expensive and there is nothing to read anyway, even if one is literate. Little that happens outside the village excites Pathuru.

True, the radio is blaring away at some distance in the main *bazaar* where the Panchayat office is, but while everyone can *hear* it, only a small group of five or six people are *listening* to it because they are interested in the news and in the rural program. When the music starts, they move away, and the Panchayat office is virtually deserted except for "Oli," the clerk whose duty it is to turn the radio on at a certain time and turn it off two hours later, for otherwise the batteries will run down.

The five or six people who listen to the radio also happen to be avid newspaper readers. Three of them subscribe to newspapers, one Urdu daily and two Telugu dailies, printed in Hyderabad and delivered in Pathuru a day or two later. These young men are also intermediaries. Their interests range from Pathuru to the United Nations, from irrigation to radioactivity. In their own questioning way, they have learned a great deal, although their formal education stopped not later than the seventh or eighth grade. There is also among them the sixty-two-year-old illiterate referred to in the first chapter as Erranna. He has gained all his knowledge from listening alone.

In addition to these active information-collectors (and disseminators) there are others who read the newspaper in Pathuru. But they read quietly and keep the information to themselves. This group includes some of the big landlords, as well as a few literate members of other categories. Their usual reading room is their own home, when they can borrow one of the five copies of newspapers which come into Pathuru. The two copies which are read by the largest number of borrowers belong to the political worker (an Urdu daily) and the cloth merchant (a Telugu daily). The latter's shop is a virtual reading room. We went in a couple of times and sat with the others, reading. Everyone read in silence, replaced the page that he had read, and quietly walked out. We inquired if this was the usual practice. "Doesn't any one talk or discuss the news, after reading it?" "No," answered the merchant. "They read whatever they are interested in and leave. Tomorrow, they will not remember the headline of the main story. I have amused myself with a few little experiments of my own." And he showed us a small stack of headlines he had collected to use in "tests" which he had administered to a few friends. He was basing his conclusion on the result of those tests.

However, in talking to some of the regular readers, we found that they did remember some items. We also found that the respondents of Pathuru seemed relatively more sure than those in Kothuru of their sources of news, perhaps because they move in limited circles. The sources are not too diffused. This was true even in the case of local news. Hence, our original feeling that there were fairly distinct groupings in communication patterns in Pathuru was reinforced.

Movie viewing is surprisingly widespread in Pathuru — especially among the male population. A visit to the city "must include at least one movie," said one of our respondents, a young man who had just got back from Hyderabad after seeing a circus. Originally a group of young men had tried to charter a bus and take their families to the circus. They failed to receive enough support to pay for the bus. So the young men cycled to Hyderabad and came back to describe the thrills. But the thrills of the circus will not make too much of an impression on those who have not seen it, although they will listen politely. Even the word "circus," for which there is no Telugu equivalent, will be forgotten. In the absence of direct and prolonged contact with a new organization or a new word, very little of anything new penetrates into the consciousness of most of Pathuru's residents. "Panchayat" is the farthest most of them can go, for example, in talking about such abstractions as "democracy" or "equality."

Although documentaries are shown in movies, few remember them. The content is as yet outside their frame of reference. While we were there, we were told that a new form of ballot, which was being used in the coming election, was explained in a documentary. Except for the political worker and two other young men, no one remembered it. Apparently, when the feature starts and the story unfolds, the movie viewer of Pathuru is all attention. Until then, he or she is talking to friends or taking care of the children who usually accompany the parents everywhere.

Schooling seems to be, as yet, an "unnecessary" thing for the children of Pathuru. The parents' attitude is reflected in the high number of truants and in the casual approach of the teachers as well. The year before we arrived there were 94 students enrolled; the number had increased to 106 at the time of our stay. On our visits to the school, however, we noticed not only the student absentees, but also the staff absentees. The average attendance, for both staff and students, is less than 75 per cent. The explanation given for this state of affairs is that the landlords, who would take an interest in the school if their own children attended it, do not do so because they send their children to Hyderabad. Pathuru only has a primary school; enrollment is fairly high because primary education is not only free but compulsory. Attendance, however, is not.

The acting headmaster during our stay in the village (the headmaster had been away on leave for over three months and had never been replaced) was twenty years old, and commanded no respect whatsoever, although he was conscientious and took seriously his job of going from house to house to enroll students under the free and compulsory scheme. When we asked one of the landlords about the state of the school and why he did not send his children there, his reply was concise: "How can I send my children to such a poor school?" It was impossible for him to understand that perhaps the school was "poor" because he was taking no interest in it, although he was one of the senior members of the Panchayat. He had left that responsibility to the district inspector of schools who had not visited Pathuru for over a year. The young acting headmaster had to do the best he could, and two days out of every month, on working days, he had to go to Ibrahimpatnam, five miles by cycle, to collect his own and his staff's salaries. On those days, for all the work that went on in the school, it might as well have been closed.

In Pathuru, as in Kothuru, we were told that there was "enthusiasm" for adult education, but no facilities. This enthusiasm was a little hard to believe in, in view of the attitude of most adults toward the education of their children. The few adults who felt differently had already made their own arrangements and learned the three R's. But they have little to read.

The average number of readers of each copy of a newspaper in Pathuru is six, including the cloth merchant's copy which has the highest readership — ten. The Panchayat office has no newspapers, no magazines, no reading room, only a few posters on the walls explaining the five-year plan, family planning, compost-pit digging, and the like. But since few villagers enter the room, the posters presumably are for the edification of the clerk and the few members of the Panchayat.

The average number of listeners to the Panchayat radio is six. There are three other radios — all battery-operated — in Pathuru, but only one of them is used by anyone other than the immediate family. News is seldom heard, except in the house of the richest landlord, and even there only he listens to it, not even the rest of the family, which consists of his wife and two small children. His other children are in the city in school and college.

The average number of letters arriving daily in the village is four. There is no telephone, and in the memory of the local sub-postmaster, there has never been a telegram delivered in the village. It would have to be delivered by a man coming from Ibrahimpatnam.

Except for the few elite, and a handful of the educated and influential intermediaries like the active political worker, the information level in Pathuru remains low. While contact with the city is widespread, it is not intense, because there is very little business for most people there. Pathuru's image of the world, therefore, is limited. It does not go too far beyond the village in space and not too far either backward or forward in time. Pathuru, for the most part, looks at itself and talks about itself; it does not like what it sees, and talks about that fact a great deal; it has so far not done much to bring about a change.

CHAPTER 3

THE DYNAMICS OF CHANGE

WHEN Edwin G. Boring said that "the single investigator works pretty much like a rat in a maze," he was perhaps not thinking of a field worker in an Indian village, but he very well could have been. He did give the rat the benefit of the doubt by adding that it works "by insight, hypothesis, trial and then error or success." [1]

Out of more or less that kind of exercise emerged the pictures of the two villages in the previous chapter. Whether we look at countries at different stages of development or at smaller communities — such as Pathuru and Kothuru — the relative poverty of the "underdeveloped" as compared with the "developed" becomes apparent in many areas. The contrasts that are apparent can serve as the bases for hypotheses. When these hypotheses are tested in the full context of social interaction and when such data are supplemented by ob-

[1] See "The Dual Role of the Zeitgeist in Scientific Creativity," in Philipp G. Frank, ed., *The Validation of Scientific Theories* (Boston: Beacon Press, 1956), p. 206.

49

servation and by responses of older citizens to questions on the progress of their community, the dynamics of change become clearer.

Pathuru and Kothuru are obviously at different stages of development. But how does one differ from the other in the various areas which impinge upon the relationship between communication and development? If we look at these several factors, does the relationship itself show up? For instance, if we know that Kothuru is more advanced than Pathuru in its habits of media use and also in its ability to take advantage of industrial opportunities and economic innovations, can we say that one led to the other? If so, in which direction? Why?

Take Ayyanna, the tailor of Kothuru. Our question to him was simple; his answer complicated. We asked him if he went to the movies often. "Yes," he said, "in fact I *have* to see every movie that comes to any town nearby." Our curiosity was aroused. His explanation was fascinating.

Unless Ayyanna saw every movie within a radius of about fifteen miles, his business was going to suffer. In fact it had picked up in the first place because of the movies. The women of Kothuru had begun to order their blouses by mentioning the name of an actress, specifying a scene in a particular movie. An order may run something like this: "Can you make me a blouse like the one Vyjayanthimala was wearing in that scene where she elopes with the landlord's son in *Modern Girl*?" Ayyanna nods his head in the affirmative, even if he has not seen the movie. He takes himself off promptly to the show. His profit on the first blouse hardly pays for his admission to the movie, but he knows that there will be other orders from other women who will point not to the actress, but to Appamma — Ayyanna's first customer.

Ayyanna's attitude toward the movies is almost entirely motivated by economic considerations. Any entertainment or other value they might have had for him under different circumstances is spoiled by the need to concentrate his attention on a specific scene. However, Ayyanna's exposure to the media is expanding. Today, he also cuts out pictures from newspapers and magazines. He is planning to buy a new sewing machine and some design books. He is also looking for an apprentice to help him.

Meanwhile the women of Kothuru continue to look upon the movies as pure entertainment, oblivious to the fact that they have at least contributed to the economic betterment of one individual in their village, and possibly more. The men of Kothuru have reacted similarly. Their shirts have collars now and an increasing number of them are emulating the styles of city folk. "In fact," says the Kothuru *karanam*, "the tailor today can't make the collarless shirt, which I find more comfortable."

It is tempting to ask if communication led to economic development in the case of Ayyanna. It might be suggested that if the women of Kothuru had not had the wherewithal to see the movies, if there had not been prior economic development, Ayyanna would not have received the orders and would not have gone to the movies himself. But then, if Ayyanna had not seen the movies, would he have been able to do so well in his trade?

The dynamics of change, therefore, are not cut and dried. But they are reasonably clear. Exposure to the media or to city-folk can trigger dormant desires, for prettier clothes, for example, creating certain demands which, in the course of time, bring their own supply. The entire process becomes clearer when small communities are observed, compared, and assessed.

We have observed Kothuru and Pathuru; now let us compare them and assess their development processes. One of the villages we have studied has developed more than the other. We are attempting to understand why. Our proposition is that communication and development are related and that the interaction is constant and cumulative. What does the evidence show?

To bring the role of communication into sharper focus within the context of the dynamics of change, a quotation from Malinowski may be helpful: "The reason why an artifact, a habit, or an idea or belief becomes permanently incorporated into a culture . . . is because it enters an instrumental series at one stage or another, and because it remains as an integral part of an instrumental series . . . a habit which is not reinforced becomes unlearned, 'extinguished,' "

51

He goes on to add that "the understanding of any cultural element must imply, among other things, the statement of its relationship, instrumental or direct, to the satisfaction of essential needs, whether these be basic, that is biological, or derived, that is cultural. When a habit ceases to be rewarded, reinforced, that is, vitally useful, it simply drops out." [2]

In looking at the findings on Kothuru's and Pathuru's attitudes, behavioral patterns, knowledge statuses, and power structure, we shall pay particular attention to this process of reinforcement or lack of it, as well as to the presence or absence of the "instrumentalities" for goal attainment. Communication, working freely in a reinforcing atmosphere, has, I believe, brought about the greater change in Kothuru. In Pathuru, many drives have been repressed on account of the absence of free communication channels, among other things. In the context of economic or political development, socially derived drives are themselves a function of communication. In order to demonstrate this, it is imperative that communication processes in Kothuru and Pathuru be made explicit and the emerging patterns charted out.

In what follows, wherever possible the contrast between the villages is shown in numerical form; the figures are derived from responses made by full-fledged members of each community to the questionnaire items. Weeded out of this part of the analysis (and only this part) are government officials, who do not psychologically and physically feel part of the village, and specialists who were interviewed for specific kinds of information, as well as for purposes of cross-checking. After the weeding-out process was completed, we were left with forty respondents (ten of them elite) for each village.

There can be no elaborate statistical analysis because at this point, in a study of this nature, when we are comparing two communities, we can only talk in terms of "more" and "less" and "higher" and "lower." We do not have any absolute measures. In Appendix I where our methods are discussed it is explained why certain tech-

[2] Bronislaw Malinowski, *A Scientific Theory of Culture* (New York: Oxford University Press, 1960), pp. 141–142.

niques were used and not others. Much the same limitations hold for reporting the findings. As Paul Neurath has said, "Just as village improvement at this point must rely largely on methods that can be handled with shovel and pickax . . . so village research must for the time being rely largely on what can be studied with the help of percentages and averages." [3] And we, of course, are not justified in applying statistical tests even to our percentages and averages.

The purpose here in presenting the data obtained from the questionnaires is simply to compare samples drawn in the field. It is interesting to note that the samples do reflect, to some degree, the overall picture which emerged from observation and inspection of official records.

Communication Patterns

Use of Media. Mass communication facilities in the developed communities, it has been shown repeatedly, are much greater than in the developing communities. Not only can people with a higher economic standard afford to subscribe to newspapers and periodicals and to buy radio sets, but the economic system is geared to meet this demand and provide effective transmitting facilities. Whether the process starts with the demand or the supply is a difficult point to settle, for it can work both ways. We can see, for instance, that the tremendous increase in the number of transistor radio sets in a country like the United States is not entirely the result of demand. Persuasive advertising has succeeded in placing more radio sets in the home than the number that can actually be used. In the developing communities, on the other hand, retarded economic progress has meant low media consumption and poor mass communication facilities. The relationship between *mass* communications and economic development is clear.

However, here we are concerned with communication in all its aspects, media and personal. In the description of the villages and their communication characteristics, both media participation and the patterns of interpersonal communication were referred to. In this

[3] Paul Neurath, "Social Research in Newly Independent Countries: An Indian Example," in *Public Opinion Quarterly*, 24:672 (Winter 1960).

total process of information flow, how do Kothuru and Pathuru compare?

Kothuru reads more newspapers, periodicals, and books, listens in larger numbers to the radio, and goes to the movies oftener than Pathuru. While it is true that because of economic development Kothuru can afford to buy more newspapers and so on, attitude differences seem to make the residents of Kothuru more curious in specific areas. These attitudes also help them to increase their knowledge. How else can one explain the larger audience for the community radio set?

It is also revealing to note that the only instance of a newspaper being read aloud to a group of illiterates was observed in Kothuru and not in Pathuru despite the latter's slower pace of life and higher illiteracy. The fact that a group of people unable to read themselves have felt the need to expose themselves to the newspaper in almost daily sessions is an indication of Kothuru's attitude which aids its growing media participation.

The reading sessions are held daily in the barber's shop. The barber himself is illiterate. So are many of his friends. But his son has been to school and can read. To the background music of busy scissors, the son reads while the father and his friends listen. Discussions usually follow. There was no such scene in Pathuru. Each one in Pathuru reads in silence; there is no discussion.

The differences between Kothuru and Pathuru are summarized in the tabulation.

USE OF MEDIA[4]

	Kothuru	Pathuru
Copies of newspapers circulating in the village	28	5
Average number of readers of each copy of a newspaper	7	6
Number of radio sets	10	4
Average daily number of listeners to the community radio set		
All programs	30	6
News programs only	5	6

[4] Because of the small number involved in newspaper reading and radio listening, it was possible to check sources and arrive at average numbers. For movie viewing this was difficult, although it was easy to observe from amount of travel to the city, and the like, that more people in Kothuru watched movies at regular intervals (at least once in six months) than in Pathuru. The fig-

Mobility. Mobility, as a factor in communication, enables a person not only to observe things outside his own community but also to interact with people who have different habits and, in some cases, speak other languages. This experience of exposing oneself to a wider area of human activity as well as interacting with people other than those whom one knows intimately leads to an increase in knowledge and a widening of horizons.

The cumulative effect of increasing mobility, of an exposure to attractive opportunities elsewhere, of the feedback that comes into the community from those who have moved or temporarily accepted jobs in a nearby city, is a general feeling of self-confidence. Once total dependence on family and immediate community is given up, one is led by stages — and very slow stages — to independent entrepreneurship. The stage of reliance on government may even be bypassed, as Kothuru seems to have done.

We have seen how the military commandant's need for certain agricultural commodities changed Kothuru's farming habits. The visits made to the city by some of Kothuru's residents in the course of this interaction, and in meeting other needs, soon brought to their attention the opportunities available in the Visakhapatnam harbor. It took a small group of enterprising young men to start the process. Today almost 250 workers in the city's harbor hail from Kothuru. They work there for six months in the year. For the other six months, as we have already seen, they come back to Kothuru, stay with their families, help in farming on their own land. Economically, they are much better off than if they merely worked on their farms eking out a meager living. In addition, they have played a major role in transforming the thinking processes of most of Kothuru's older residents.

Pathuru has tried this experiment too. Unfortunately, however, it has failed — at least for the time being. A small group of young laborers had heard somewhere that there were good opportunities for jobs in the cities, especially in the industrial city of Bombay.

ures as obtained from our respondents were 73 per cent and 60 per cent respectively. But it seems likely that the difference is even higher than that because of the higher amount of travel on the part of Kothuru's non-elite as compared with Pathuru's.

55

They collected what little money they could and left. Little had they realized that one does not just walk into a mill and get a job; nor did they realize that a totally different language was spoken in Bombay and that a big, busy, sprawling city like this has little time to take care of the personal difficulties of a group of villagers from Pathuru. They traveled about 1000 miles to be disillusioned and disheartened. (One wonders why they went that far instead of seeking jobs in Hyderabad.) Letters have come back to Pathuru from most of these young men asking for money for the train fare back home. All of Pathuru knows this and the pathetic letters from these pioneers have been enough to convince the villagers, except the few well educated, that the city is bad and that the only place for them is home — i.e., Pathuru.

At least to some extent this might explain why so few of our respondents from Pathuru had traveled beyond Hyderabad, while so many of the Kothuru residents had traveled beyond Visakhapatnam. If we treat as highly mobile those who had traveled beyond the nearest city, Kothuru's percentage in this category, as judged from our sample, was 62.5 and Pathuru's 15. Few of even the elite of Pathuru had ventured beyond Hyderabad but several of our respondents in Kothuru had gone as far as Delhi. Three of them, who were by no means richer than some of Pathuru's leading citizens, had only recently completed an all-India tour on an attractive railway scheme worked out by the Indian Railways to encourage the public to "see your country." It is doubtful if anyone in Pathuru had even heard of the scheme.

Today many of Kothuru's residents are sending their children to high schools and technical schools in Visakhapatnam and elsewhere; the farthest that most of Pathuru's older children go is to Ibrahimpatnam, five miles away. The only exceptions are the sons of two of Pathuru's richest landlords. They are studying in Hyderabad and living in their parents' "city house," complete with servants.

The women of Pathuru summarize most adequately the over-all attitude: "Oh, if we send our children to the big city, we don't know who will see them and what they will do to them!" Mobility, under these conditions, is hard. Such an attitude doesn't necessarily keep *everyone* home; but then it does not encourage enough people to "see your country," either.

Interpersonal Communication. With increasing use of the media, greater travel, and a faster pace of life, a developing community generally has less time to spend in interpersonal communication. At the same time, the interpersonal communication that does take place is far less restricted than that in a traditional community.

In the early stages of development the elite and the mass of the people are separated by a wide gap, not only in terms of their material resources, but in their knowledge and attitudes in the social and political spheres. The elite tend to be more knowledgeable, cosmopolitan, and politically informed. The mass, on the other hand, are almost totally illiterate, tradition-bound, and seemingly impervious to change. Whereas the elite may have traveled and even been educated in institutions of higher learning, and have developed the capacity to think and act in ways other than what their fathers and grandfathers did, the mass's only yardstick is the past. While the mass, generally, seek the security of the past, the elite seek the promise of the future and are prepared for a policy of change even if they are not agreed among themselves about what shape such change ought to take.

Thus in thought and action, in attitudes and behavior, the elite are separated from the mass. Change is initiated by the few, understood by the few, and even used by the few — until the natural process of communication takes these ideas of the few to the many and whatever benefits may accrue slowly begin to be shared. Communication must bridge this gulf before a whole community can develop evenly. And this process has to work in such a way that the elite come closer to the mass and vice versa.

Kothuru and Pathuru show some of these differences between the developed community and the traditional. The difference in the *amount* of interpersonal communication is not too great. What is striking is the *pattern*.

The time spent in interpersonal communication is greater in Pathuru, where the pace of life is much slower, the channels of communication fewer, and travel and entertainment are acutely limited.

The residents of Pathuru, therefore, spend a great deal of time sitting in groups and talking, especially after dusk. There is little movement in the dark village square, lit only by a small oil lamp burning inside the Panchayat office and another small lamp in the teashop. About six people sit in the square for an hour or so listening to the Panchayat radio. A little after 7:00 P.M. the square is virtually deserted. Within the village, small groups of people sit on verandas if the evening is warm, or just inside the main door if it is cool outside. Since everyone goes to bed early, by about 7:30, the talking does not last late. However, in the fields the next day, the same topic can be taken up and continued.

Kothuru's pattern of communication differs from this. There is less time for long chats. But, since mobility is high, the contacts are spread over a wider area, both in the main part of the village and at the "junction." People spend less time talking, but talk to more people and a greater variety of individuals during any single day. Pathuru's communication is limited to specific groups, whereas Kothuru's is much freer. This greater diffusion enables Kothuru to get more information from more sources even through interpersonal communication than Pathuru is able to achieve despite the amount of time it spends talking.

Another important difference lies in the interaction between the elite and the mass. Kothuru's elite move far more easily and readily in the village, and interact more with the ordinary people; the latter feel free to stop and talk to the landlord or the Panchayat president or even a government official. In Pathuru, however, not only do the elite shut themselves up, but on the few occasions when they do walk in the village, the ordinary people move aside as though they have no right to be walking on the same road as the "big man."

How do the elite respondents themselves feel about this? Do they really talk to more people now than they used to? Yes, said every elite respondent in Kothuru. Only 50 per cent of the elite respondents believed this to be the case in Pathuru. One of them, a younger member of the elite, was quite candid about it: "These days, one has to. We have to seek their vote sometimes." Among those who did not think they talked to more people than at an earlier time, two replies were interesting. One said, "Why should we talk to those illiterates? They will not understand us anyway." Another said: "We don't have to — not even for elections. They have to vote for us. We have been their leaders since their grandfathers' time."

The elite-mass interaction will be referred to later in this chapter. Suffice now to note that Kothuru's residents talk more freely among themselves irrespective of socioeconomic differences than Pathuru's. Hence, the sources of information are wider in Kothuru whether one takes only the media into consideration or adds to them the various ways in which information can flow through human interaction — at home, at work, on the road, in the restaurant, and in buses.

Source of News. We have seen that Kothuru's media participation is higher than Pathuru's. But to what extent does Kothuru rely on the media as sources of news? How does it compare with Pathuru? Does a developing community show a greater reliance on the media as compared with the traditional?

The distinction here between the two villages is not as clear-cut as in interpersonal communication. Both the villages still rely very heavily on oral communication. The media play a minor role as sources of *direct* information, even for those who can read. When we take the percentage of illiteracy in both villages into consideration, we can, of course, understand why the media play a minor role. But when we find that even the literate do not often cite the media as sources of news, we have to seek a full explanation elsewhere.

Economic conditions are certainly one reason. Not all literates can afford to buy, say, a newspaper. Many borrow, but borrowing has its limitations. The library copies are available, but when the library is open, most people are at work. Also, since political news is not of much interest to the typical villager, he finds the newspaper rather dull.

As for the radio, news programs are broadcast at a specific time in the evening. The one program in the regional language lasts fifteen minutes. Even this is found to be unintelligible to many because of its "high-class" Telugu.

Both the radio and the newspaper concentrate heavily on national news. State news comes second and local news is almost totally absent unless it is something really big, in which case the chances are that most people have already heard about it.

One other important reason for the lack of a clear-cut distinction in our findings between Kothuru and Pathuru in the role of the media as sources of information is that the questions in the information part of our questionnaire which specifically asked for the source of each of several items failed to elicit clear responses. Regular readers of newspapers or listeners to the radio named their source, but the casual reader more often than not merely said he had "heard it somewhere." To the extent that Kothuru had more readers and listeners, it stood slightly higher than Pathuru in the number of times the media were cited as primary sources. In actual fact the difference may be bigger, but this requires further study with more refined tools.

Information Level. When it came to information level, however, the difference between Kothuru and Pathuru was quite clear, both in the responses to questions that were part of the questionnaire itself and in responses to questions in casual conversation about such matters as cost of living in the city as compared with the village, bus fares, wages in industry and agriculture, price of commodities. Kothuru had ready knowledge; Pathuru was either incapable of thinking in such terms or fumbled for answers and then made some vague guesses. Even an illiterate woman worker in a rice mill in Kothuru could tell us how much quarry labor was paid for how many hours of work. Kothuru's residents are making decisions in a competitive money economy, and information about such things as wage levels is extremely important if they are to make the right decision.

Kothuru's information level then was high in areas of immediate interest to it. This is true, perhaps, the world over. But Pathuru's backwardness shows up clearly in this regard. Even on the one topic which seems to be dearest to its heart — land — it had little factual information, only a host of baseless opinions or fond hopes. This, of course, refers to the mass of the people. The elite, both in Pathuru and Kothuru, displayed a fairly high knowledge of general news.

The large majority of people in both villages were not interested in state, national, or international news.

The communication patterns in the two villages are perhaps most clearly shown by the fact that while every single person in our Kothuru sample had heard of the local news item we used in the questionnaire, almost 30 per cent of our respondents in Pathuru had not done so. In both the villages, the item referred to a natural phenomenon which had been given a religious or mystical significance by the villagers. In Kothuru it was lightning which had struck a nearby hill and created what seemed like a road. The villagers' story was that one of their most popular deities had decided to move from his present abode in a city far from the village to the top of the hill, and that the road was his work. The news first came from a nearby village. In Pathuru, the local item concerned a mammoth ceremony organized by priests and attended by over a thousand people from surrounding villages. Its purpose was to prevent by prayer the end of the world which the meeting of eight planets in the skies supposedly foreshadowed. The ceremony was held in a nearby village and was attended by priests from Pathuru.

In both villages, therefore, the news had to travel by word of mouth from a nearby village, enter the village, and there be disseminated to the rest of the village. In Kothuru it traveled much faster and was disseminated more widely than in Pathuru. In the context of Pathuru's social structure and the nature of its interpersonal communication patterns, the fact that the local news item was not carried to some segments in the village is understandable. So is the result in Kothuru where interpersonal communication is highly diffused, both vertically and horizontally.

State news apparently evokes little interest in either village. National news does slightly better and international news was recalled by a considerably larger number in Kothuru, though many of the villagers there could not follow the scientific aspect of the testing of the atomic bomb (the effects of radioactivity). Response on the economic item on our questionnaire (knowledge of life insurance) was second only to the local item in both villages, though the difference between them was still quite striking. Over 80 per cent of our respondents in Kothuru knew reasonably well the details of life insurance; in Pathuru, only 50 per cent.

Ability to Cope with New Ideas and Things. On the basis of such varied measures as information level, media participation, and interpersonal communication, it was possible to gauge the difference between Pathuru and Kothuru in desire or willingness to learn about new things and to grapple with new ideas, whether these pertained mainly to jobs and consumer goods or to topics ranging from radioactivity to fertilizer, from democracy to the local Panchayat.

While Kothuru's residents interacted with a wide range of people of all occupations and socioeconomic levels, talked about a great number of things, listened with interest to conversation on a wide variety of subjects, and inquired intelligently into some aspects of subjects they were not familiar with, Pathuru's residents were more inclined to talk than to listen, to confine this talk to small groups (not necessarily based on caste, but largely in predictable cliques) and to a narrow range of topics, especially land and village gossip. In prolonged conversations with respondents of both villages, we learned far more about Pathuru in the first few days than about Kothuru in the first few weeks. This was because Pathuru's residents were more inclined to talk about their village and their grievances than Kothuru's. The latter were more keen on asking questions and clarifying certain thoughts which may have occurred to them during their talks with us. This was also true of their general attitude in conversations with the wide variety of people they interacted with, whether in their work situation or in social relationships.

As an example of the difference between Kothuru and Pathuru one might take the contrasting ways those in the two villages responded when they were asked if they had heard of Russia's testing the 50-megaton bomb. If a person in Kothuru had *not* heard of it, or of its evil effects, he would ask questions about when it was tested and why. The typical Pathuru resident would say that he had not heard about it and go on to talk about the "police action" which occurred in Hyderabad following the partition of India and how people killed each other or ran from the police during those terrible days. His interest in the bomb ended with the question, but the question itself triggered something in his memory about the past and about the village. His interest was in telling what he knew, not in learning what he did not know. The lack of stimulants from outside, perhaps, had made him fall back upon his own resources and all he could talk about that was stimulating was what he himself knew or had experienced. He could also talk about what he wanted to know, but this was confined to the subject of land. He wanted to know whether and when the government was going to give him some more land. He had heard rumors about plans for land redistribution, but he had heard them from others in his group who also had no definite knowledge. Instead of finding sources which would help them clarify their doubts (as Kothuru residents might do), they talked about the matter at great length. Few issues are closed in Pathuru; therefore, the limited number of issues within its frame of reference become perennial topics of conversation. The resident of Kothuru, on the other hand, shows greater ability to seek solutions to present problems and then to seek new avenues for action.

Knowledge of Technical Subject Matter. By exposing himself to a wider circle of people and things, the typical Kothuru resident has acquired a greater knowledge of technical subject matter than his counterpart in Pathuru. When technical subject matter is referred to in the context of Indian village life, it must be remembered that if a villager can talk about such basic things as compost pits, oil or electric engines that pump water out of his well, ammonium sulphate in connection with fertilizer, D.D.T., and the like, he is displaying a relatively high amount of technical knowledge. He does not have to talk of the thrust of a jet engine or the horsepower of an automobile. In the course of displaying such knowledge, he is automatically using words which are comparatively new to him and his community, and words which have been borrowed from another language, although some of them do have cumbersome translations in the local language. The villager learns these words in talks with government officials, and the latter find it far more convenient to use the original word as they had first learned it in their own reading or training than to make the effort to learn the vernacular equivalent. It is true that posters printed at the state headquarters do use the translation. But the number of people who see these posters is very limited. In any case, before the posters ever come into the village, many residents have already heard the foreign word and made it part of their vocabulary.

The speed with which some of these words have become part of Kothuru's vocabulary is an indication of its ability to absorb technical subject matter. To the villager who but a few years ago could only refer to any motor-driven vehicle as "motor car" the different terms used for jeeps, trucks, buses, and automobiles, as well as motorcycles and scooters, now come equally naturally. So do terms such as "factory," "injection," "telephone," "minister," "M.L.A." (member of the legislative assembly) — all in their English form.

Kothuru's residents have been directly exposed to all these objects, including the minister and the M.L.A. However, it would be stretching the point too far to suggest that they know the exact nature of the duties of these dignitaries. They come and go and people talk about them a little, and forget. But not so the factory, the engine, the ammonium sulphate, and the Block, for these are constantly in the thoughts of the villagers and they know exactly what each does. To that extent, the knowledge of Kothuru's residents has advanced considerably in the last few years.

Pathuru presents a similar picture, but the advance is much less, for the exposure has been much less. Still, Pathuru too has taken into its vocabulary terms such as "injection," "electricity" (about which there is some talk in the village), "bus." The difference in degree, however, is great. Although an M.L.A. or two have visited the village at election time, no one remembers them, even by name, let alone their designation, for the M.L.A. usually meets a few of the elite and leaves. The average villager has no way of knowing who the man was. There are few who will try and explain it to him, in contrast to Kothuru where the elite take the visitor around and make him address a meeting. The Kothuru elite have the desire to show off their village and let the villagers see the leader. In short, the elite in Kothuru have respect for the average villager, whereas in Pathuru the elite are satisfied if they merely entertain the visiting leader. The Pathuru elite are neither proud of the village nor interested in increasing the knowledge of the mass.

This difference in attitude has a direct effect on the flow of technical knowledge in Pathuru. The little that the elite know does not flow down. Hence the sources of new words or of technical subject matter are limited. The lack of direct exposure to new things adds to the gulf of difference between the two villages. Pathuru does not have as many engines or factories or a telephone. Also, as we have seen, travel is limited and the attitude toward the gaining of more knowledge is negative. In the absence of both the desire to learn and the facilities to observe, Pathuru lags behind.

Some of the new words which have entered the vocabulary of the non-elite in Kothuru are interesting. They include such things as "compulsory" (probably because primary education is compulsory; vaccination is compulsory), "scheme" (everything the government official does is part of some scheme or other). From the lips of the elite, they would not sound so incongruous.

In our curiosity, we asked several villagers if they knew the meanings of these words. They did, and explained them to us. But they did not know that these were English words! They used them in the proper place in a string of Telugu words. One illiterate farmer who also used the words "information" and "loan" was surprised when we told him that they were not Telugu words.

The radio announcer, and to a lesser degree the newspaper editor, continue to translate their material into literary Telugu, and then the villager — in both Kothuru and Pathuru — is at a loss. He loses interest in the news programs and listens to the music instead. The number of villagers who mentioned unintelligibility as the reason for not listening to the radio was so high that one cannot but hope that radio announcers will learn some "new words" which the villager does understand.

Level of Abstract Thought. Kothuru's lead over Pathuru was also visible in level of abstraction achieved. Kothuru residents showed greater capacity to think and talk abstractly.

While it was possible to judge this purely through observation and by listening to our respondents, a very simple device was used in the field to measure abstract thinking—a five-point scale on which each respondent was ranked after our last conversation with him or her. Each respondent's score depended on the content of his conversation with us and his answers to specific questions. For example, if throughout the dialogue, a respondent could only refer to the Panchayat president as Mr. Naidu, to the Block Development Officer as Mr. Raman, and so on, he was judged as being capable of thinking in less abstract terms than those who used the term "Panchayat" or at progressively higher levels the terms "village self-government," "self-government," and finally "democracy." A respondent who reached the highest level of abstraction received the score of 5. The ranking was done on the basis of the total conversation and not on the discussion of any given topic. Levels of abstraction could be estimated for "planning," "politics," "equality," etc.

The difference between Kothuru and Pathuru emerged after all the questionnaires were completed and the abstract thinking scores were analyzed, as shown in the tabulation.

NUMBER REACHING EACH LEVEL OF ABSTRACT THINKING

	Kothuru	Pathuru
First level	1	1
Second level	3	10
Third level	7	8
Fourth level	9	13
Fifth level	20	8

Patterns of Attitude

It is clear that Kothuru has more sources of information than Pathuru and that it uses them far more effectively. It is better informed. That much is easy to see and show. However, we would also like to know how it uses this information and what good it has achieved. Attitude is important here.

Attitude toward Change. Thanks to the information that it has within its own boundaries and to the confidence it has that any other information it may need can be easily obtained, Kothuru moves more resolutely than Pathuru. It has the initial advantage of a broader horizon. It has too the knowledge that this horizon can be extended if need be—beyond Visakhapatnam, beyond the state itself if necessary. This is what makes it curious, questioning, free, and willing. It is possible for Kothuru to assess in its own manner some of the ways of the outside world and adapt to the changes that it knows are inevitable.

Kothuru has felt the changes that have already occurred and is fully conscious of them. It points to the changes with pride and freely admits that more change is on the way. It is ready for it and will even welcome it. Not so Pathuru. "What changes are there?" it asks. "Things are as they have been for years. In some areas, they are getting worse, that's all."

In the total set of attitudes that a developing community might show, perhaps consciousness of change is the most significant. For only when that consciousness is present will the community be able to think in terms of the possibility of change, seek knowledge to find out about the avenues for change, and then act in ways that will turn change to its own advantage.

The attitude that is important in this case is not merely an apathetic acquiescence or a detached view of change as it is occurring somewhere else, but an active feeling that one is part of this change.

Both Kothuru and Pathuru have seen changes within the villages themselves as well as in the cities which so many of the residents have visited; they have also directly experienced some changes. For example, some new shops have been opened in the villages, buses run through the villages, movies have been shown in places not far from the villages and the villagers have sat through them, some visitors who have come to the villages have dressed differently and even talked differently, elections have been held with all the attendant campaigning. It is true that some of these changes have occurred in Kothuru more rapidly and in larger measure than in Pathuru. However, that by itself cannot explain the vast divergence in opinion regarding change; nor does it explain, to one who has lived in both the villages, the feeling one gets that while Kothuru is ready to take advantage of all the opportunities that change brings, Pathuru is sitting back waiting for free land or for doles. It does not seek out opportunities as Kothuru is prepared to do. Basically, it does not know what to do or where to turn. Communication channels are either blocked or suspect.

In Kothuru, most people, rich or poor, readily point out *concrete* changes. They do not talk in abstractions such as democracy or even village self-government, government plans or nationhood, but they can count off the number of new shops, the number of new houses, the exact increase in the number of bus services to the city, as well as discuss the changes in dress styles, eating habits, and the like. The Pathuru villager is unable to talk even about concrete changes, although new shops have been opened, bus services have been inaugurated, and dress styles have changed. The typical Pathuru villager has to be probed before conceding that "all these things" did not exist five years ago.

Kothuru's sense of change could be felt in its speed of life and its readiness to grasp opportunities whether at the individual level (opening a new shop to cater to new tastes and demands) or at the collective level through the Panchayat (laying plans to construct a new school building worth Rs. 30,000). Pathuru's sense of change cannot be felt until one talks to the handful of young aspirants and the few educated landlords. The sense of change has not permeated down to the mass of the people. Hence change itself has been slow and uneven. Only the few who are conscious of it have taken advantage of opportunities and they have done so quietly and for themselves.

The few young men who would like to see these changes work for the betterment of the community are as yet powerless to do much except make the mass even more discontented. While this discontent could very well be the first step toward more active participation in change, the avenues for such action are not visible to most people.

Both Kothuru and Pathuru could express themselves only in mainly economic terms when asked whether any perceptible change had occurred in the villages during the last several years. Few of the respondents referred to any social or political changes spontaneously. If this may be taken as an indication of the people's priorities, it augurs well for economic development, as well as for the absorption of information directly concerning possibilities for economic improvement. Both these were evident in Kothuru; both were less evident in Pathuru.

It is interesting and significant that the sense-of-change variable separates the elite from the mass almost dramatically in Pathuru. There is no such break in attitudes in Kothuru. The elite-mass gap and the elite's gatekeeper role in information processes were both brought home sharply in responses to questions on changes in the villages. Ninety per cent of the elite of Kothuru displayed a high sense of change, compared with 80 per cent in Pathuru; but when it came to the non-elite sample, the figure for Kothuru remained almost as high while that for Pathuru fell to less than 25 per cent.

This is understandable. For when we define change as consisting of those factors which go into making rapid development possible, we are at once talking of what people know, how people react to what they know, what people see, and how they react to what they see. To what extent then is consciousness of change a result of communication? Most underdeveloped communities, as already noted, are communications poor. Therefore change is little noticed whether it occurs in the nearby metropolis or in some distant place. Where communications are poor (here I refer to both travel facilities and media) most communities within the larger universe are isolated. Under such conditions, change has to occur from within and any ideas that grow ought to germinate locally. This is bound to be an extremely slow and ineffective process. If some communication channels are available, these are limited, at the start, to a few rich and influential people. The village headman may meet a visitor from outside or the local landlord may take a trip to the nearest city. Since communication at the early stages is almost entirely horizontal, whatever new things are noticed or discussed remain solely within the purview of the small clique of elite. Acceptance of the change for themselves or any attempt to bring about change in others may be detrimental to their own interest. Change, therefore, seldom is encouraged. Any latent desire to change is likely to be quelled, for there are so few who know what it means and the first ones who know are its worst enemies, in their own interest.

69

Education in Pathuru is a good example. Normally, in any developing community, education is recognized as an asset. Those who get the better jobs are those who are better educated. Parents will go to great lengths to send their children to school. But this is not so in Pathuru. The few rich landlords have sent their children to school in the city, while Pathuru's own school languishes for want of support. The landlords are not interested, for their own children do not attend this school. The richest landlord of the village said he did not send his children to the village school because it was "no good." The headmaster of the school said it was difficult to run the school because the landlords gave it no support, either moral or financial. It is entirely government-supported.

Kothuru, on the other hand, sees the necessity for good education. It knows that new opportunities are more readily available to the educated. Even the illiterate parents are conscious of this and send their children to school. There are two schools in Kothuru (primary and secondary) for 315 regular students. The wealthier parents who can afford it send their older children to high schools or technical schools in Visakhapatnam and elsewhere. Pathuru has one school (primary) for 106 students enrolled, of whom only about 80 attend on an average day.

The women of Pathuru again summarize Pathuru's attitude toward education. "Will education feed our children? They are more useful at home or on the farms." Kothuru knows that education will feed its children and feed them better — in the long run. Kothuru can think in terms of the long run. Pathuru cannot.

Attitude toward the Future. Kothuru has widened its horizons, not only spatially but temporally. It is able to separate the past, the present, and the future and to think in these terms. "If it was good enough for my grandfather, it's good enough for me" is an indication of traditionalism. Unless one has the ability to look into the future by sizing up the present in relation to the past, the growth potential is bound to be limited.

A second aspect of this is empathy. Variously defined by various people, empathy is essentially an ability to put oneself in another's shoes. Used in the figurative sense, it becomes an aspect of "future

70

orientation," for it involves both time and space. Only if a person believes that he too can become the village headman some day can he talk as though he were already wearing the incumbent's shoes. This sense of potential gives one confidence to plan for the future. One who cannot imagine himself in the headman's shoes will probably remain the son of his father, the village blacksmith.

Needless to say, if one has not heard of the office of chief minister he can hardly be expected to put himself in that dignitary's shoes. The basic difference in knowledge and in perception of change which separates Kothuru and Pathuru automatically separates them in their "future orientation" and in their ability to empathize.

"Future orientation" as a phrase can be interpreted in at least two ways. It can stand for the ability of an individual to project and to plan for the future. It can also stand for the attitude an individual shows in his thoughts and actions which indicates some optimism or pessimism about the future. Whatever plans he may make or whatever approaches he uses to his problems will depend importantly on his ability to project as well as on the information he has on which to base his projection.

Questions designed to elicit answers ranging from reactions to changes in the village to comments on the exact nature of a respondent's plans for the future (for himself, his sons, and his daughters) helped us judge Kothuru's and Pathuru's attitudes in this regard.

For example, Bashir Ahmed of Pathuru, who says he is looking for some way of borrowing money to expand his little cycle shop, is showing potential for entrepreneurship as well as an optimism that does not seem to exist in Akkayya, a farmer of the same village who says, "How can I save any money? The little I can will soon be used for my daughter's marriage." Or a question like "What are you planning for yourself?" put to Sathyanna of Kothuru brings the reply, "What can I plan for myself? I will just do my work and continue to live as I am living — God willing." Ranga Rao, the young Kothuru goldsmith, however, answers the same question differently. "I am hoping to study some more if there is some way of finding a school where one does not have to pay fees, or if I can get a scholarship." As an artisan he is unhappy, though skillful at his work.

Generally, though with individual exceptions as noted above, the residents of Kothuru are looking forward to a future with confidence and planning for it, each in his own way, whereas those of Pathuru are not clear about their future. Hence whatever planning the latter do is for the immediately foreseeable "emergencies" such as a daughter's marriage.

This attitude in Pathuru is understandable, because the villagers are not quite clear even about the changes that have already taken place. They lack the information sources which can explain things to them. Under such conditions, projection into a future is almost impossible. Most of Pathuru's residents are bewildered and their only way out seems to be to cling to the past and do as their fathers did — buy a little gold whenever possible and hide it in a niche in the wall. It can be taken and sold when need arises.

The typical individual in Kothuru, on the other hand, spends most of the money he earns, saves a little in the post office, or even goes so far as to invest in a life insurance policy. Even if he does not save a great deal, the confidence he has that he will find work to do makes him less resigned than the residents of Pathuru. In projecting himself into a future, the Kothuru resident seeks information on avenues available to him; the Pathuru resident is resigned to his traditional vocation as well as his traditional poverty, and cannot think of seeking information.

Ability to Empathize. This same combination of knowledge and confidence in the future also makes the Kothuru resident more empathic. Literate or illiterate, every person who was fairly well informed and displayed confidence in the future also showed himself to be empathic.

In attempting to find out to what extent empathy was present among the residents of the two villages, we did not intend to try to isolate the factors that help a person develop this capacity. However, as the questionnaires were being administered and informal interaction was taking place between investigator and respondents, it became obvious that several factors besides information or knowledge were involved in empathy. Our tools and time did not permit us to go deeper into this but it was interesting to note that several illiterates displayed a remarkable capacity to empathize, all the way from the village level to the national level.

There were three levels at which we tested our respondents' ability to empathize: the village, the state, and the nation. In each case, the respondent was to put himself in the shoes of the head of the administration. The tabulation shows the results of our inquiry.

NUMBER REACHING EACH LEVEL OF EMPATHY

	Kothuru	Pathuru
First level (village) ..	4	13
Second level (state) ..	3	0
Third level (national) .	26	18
No empathy	7	9

Comparison of these figures with those on information level confirms our conclusion that something besides knowledge is involved in empathy. Among the additional factors would seem to be positive attitudes, especially those pertaining to "future orientation" and satisfaction with life in the village; such attitudes mean that the individual is conscious of his ability to improve himself and that he has confidence that the future will be brighter than the present. There were a few among our respondents who were almost aggressive in their responses to the questions on empathy and highly critical of the present. These disgruntled persons, however, had tremendous confidence that they would "set things right." This intense feeling of being masters of their own destiny certainly carried them into the simulated role of prime minister of India without any difficulty.

One of them was Janganna, an illiterate well-digger of Pathuru, who was perhaps the most disgruntled man in the village. He was also ill informed and an active carrier of rumor — especially bits of "news" which reflected badly on the village leaders' ability to spend community money impartially. Despite the handicap of lack of knowledge, Janganna fit himself into the prime minister's shoes readily and spoke with great eloquence on how the head of the country should govern so that the poor could eat and live.

On the other hand, the educated *karanam* of Pathuru could not even reach the second level — that of the chief minister of the state. His view of the future was bleak, his view of the present one of utter

73

disgust at the "stupid masses" aspiring to things they did not deserve. He looked at the past with nostalgia. "Those were wonderful days!"

The most striking difference between Kothuru and Pathuru in responses to the empathy questions was that Kothuru's respondents were better able to suggest specific action programs while Pathuru's respondents talked in generalities. Where a Kothuru resident might say that more industry should be brought into the village, his counterpart in Pathuru would suggest that the "people's welfare" should be taken care of. Kothuru villagers suggested education, irrigation, and so on. Only a few in Pathuru referred to the need for electricity and for education. These were, in most cases, the elite.

It was not surprising that more respondents in Kothuru than in Pathuru could reach the third level. Most of them were conscious of change, more were literate and knowledgeable, more were satisfied with their own economic condition and looked forward to better things. They were also confident that they could do better because they knew what to do and where to go for information on things they were unsure of. Pathuru was less blessed with all these attitudes and facilities.

In Kothuru the elite's confidence has rubbed off on the mass, thanks to greater interpersonal contacts between the two; in Pathuru even the elite, though empathic, lacked the confidence necessary to look forward to a future with hope, and the mass, in the absence of any close contact with the elite, could not even share the knowledge that the elite possessed and which might have given them some hope. For the mass are more likely to become hopeful with even a slight increase in income or opportunity than the elite to whom such slight increases may mean little, for they are more concerned with guarding what they have, whether it is material wealth or political power or social status.

Economic and Social Patterns

Industrialization. The concern of its elite to preserve what they have may be one of the reasons why Pathuru does not have any industry as yet. The wealth of the community is concentrated in the hands of a few rich landlords. They are the only ones who can invest in new ventures. But if they do, they will need workers. These will have to come from the agricultural labor force, which is underemployed and remains readily available (for, as was noted earlier, few think of leaving the village and finding jobs elsewhere) when there is work to be done on the landlords' farms. This suits the landlords, for in a noncompetitive situation as it exists in Pathuru, labor comes cheap. If industry were to be brought in, as in Kothuru, the available labor force would diminish and wages would have to go up. A farm worker in Pathuru today, as indicated above, gets Rs. 0.50 for a day's work (usually its equivalent in grain) while his counterpart in Kothuru has to be promised at least Rs. 1.25 before he even considers the offer. Why should he work for less when his services can be offered to a tile factory, a bone mill, a quarry, transport trade, rice mills, etc. — and if all fails, there is always Visakhapatnam. During the busy season in Kothuru, it is not unusual for a farm worker to get Rs. 2.00 or more per day. In Pathuru there is no such thing as shortage of labor. The wages, therefore, can still be determined by the employer.

Kothuru has far more occupations represented within its borders than Pathuru, and the residents have considerable choice as the list of major occupations given below indicates.

MAJOR OCCUPATIONS REPRESENTED

Kothuru	*Pathuru*
Landlords	Landlords
Farmers and farm labor	Farmers and farm labor
Mill owners and staff (full time)	Mill owners and workers (part time)
Retail shops (30)	Retail shops (18)
Artisans (traditional)	Artisans (traditional)
Quarry labor	Bunding (canal) labor
Contractors and staff	
Railway workers	
Office peons	
Tile factory workers-trainees	
Bone mill workers	
Horn products workers-trainees	

75

In addition to these, Kothuru has a librarian, a newspaper vendor, a postmaster and his staff, and a gas station attendant, which Pathuru does not have. Several government officials are in residence in Kothuru, none in Pathuru.

Despite this vast difference, however, Kothuru, like Pathuru, still depends largely on agriculture, and whatever industrial development has taken place has been due to agriculture. Profits from agriculture have been invested in the village in the form of rice mills. Government-sponsored training and production centers came later. Pathuru's rich landlords have not invested anything in the village. They have taken their money into the city banks, invested in stocks and shares, and so on. Only recently has a government project opened up some work opportunities for a few of the underemployed of Pathuru. Close to the village, a bund is being built to divert the water from a nearby tank to irrigate some land in the area.

The tabulation below, based on the official census figures for 1961 (with the limitations noted in the description of Kothuru), shows the contrast in work patterns between Kothuru and Pathuru.[5] In addition to Kothuru's greater concentration than Pathuru in nonagricultural and nonhousehold industry, there is in the figures another indication of Kothuru's greater progress: the smaller percentage of workers in the total population points to the fact that a larger number of Kothuru's women have become housewives and more of its children are at school.

Having tasted the fruits of industrialization, Kothuru yearns for more; not having been exposed to them, Pathuru fears the unknown

WORK PATTERNS

	Kothuru	Pathuru
Total population	2992	2617
Working population	41.24%	52.54%
Workers in agriculture and household industry	71.15%	80.36%
Workers in nonagricultural and nonhousehold industry	28.85%	19.64%
Male workers	71.48%	59.85%
Female workers	28.52%	40.15%

[5] The figures were supplied by the Superintendent of Census Operations, Hyderabad.

and fumbles for answers when asked if it would like to see industry come into the village. Its attitude toward industrialization has not been formed. However, when the term "industrialization" is explained to the residents of Pathuru, especially in the sense that it would open up greater opportunities for jobs, they readily agree that it would be good. Once it was explained, all our respondents in Pathuru, except one, approved of industrialization. There was no exception in Kothuru. The single exception in Pathuru was the *karanam*, whose reply was: "I don't know, it might be for the better, or it might be for the worse!" The only difference between the two villages, then, lies in the fact that Kothuru needs no explanation to approve of industrialization; Pathuru needs to be told what it means.

This difference in attitude, which could only be measured by the tone of the responses (rather than the final content), showed up clearly the need for information in Pathuru, in order to dispel the hesitancy of the people, recruit them into new jobs, and aid in the reduction of pressure on land. There was no doubt that information could change attitudes. In the course of administering the questionnaire itself a change was frequently visible. For after making a mental note of a respondent's initial hesitation, we talked about what industrialization meant and what kinds of industry could be brought into Pathuru ("if only the rich landlords could be made to feel the need for it," for they alone had the money to invest and labor was plentiful). Respondents then talked at length and it did not take them long to see what the benefits could be.

Rigidity of Occupational and Social Structure. With increasing knowledge of economic opportunities on the part of Kothuru residents and increasing desire to take advantage of them has come an increasing spirit of competition. Ready information sources have helped in this process and industry itself has been helped by effective communication. The rice mills of Kothuru, for instance, have attracted farmers from many of the surrounding villages; one of the men who opened one of Kothuru's flourishing rice mills came from Pitapuram, a city far from Kothuru; the restaurant owner too came from a distance. Pathuru cannot point to one "outsider" who has decided to open a business there.

The difference between a traditional community with its fixed roles and an industrializing community with new roles for which there are no set rules lies in the openness of avenues for advancement. The rigid caste-occupation pattern of Hindu society is likely to lead to a sense of fatalism about the individual's place in the hierarchy. Usually this is reflected in a state of apathy or passive contentment which is not conducive to development. In a country like India, religion reinforces the belief that contentment is a virtue. Business activities, including the lending of money for interest, are confined to a particular caste. The people are supposedly born into the caste they deserve, including the Brahmin who is the repository of all learning and the Harijan who is the outcast destined to spend his life doing the most menial of all jobs.

Before a person can be taught to believe that his station in life is what he makes of it — essential in the development of individual initiative — he has to be exposed to new ideas, learn of people who *have* crossed the "birth barrier" and of opportunities for him to attempt the same thing. Only then can he feel the healthy discontent that stirs people to strive for new roles and for betterment of their own prospects.

Kothuru demonstrates the changes from traditionalism to modernization — a faster pace of life, an adoption of new norms, the virtual breakdown of the caste-occupation code, a spirit of self-help, and the beginnings of an implied recognition of the fact that one is, to a greater or lesser extent, the master of his own destiny and responsible for his own actions. Out of all this has grown a fairly sizable area of entrepreneurship.

Pathuru, as we have seen, is still backward in all of these areas. Economic growth, social change, and political maturity, as a result, have suffered.

Unless people are willing to take risks and invest in new ideas for production and distribution of goods and services, economic growth is bound to be slow. To bring about conditions conducive to the development of such individuals, knowledge of market potential and of avenues of investment is essential. Capital alone does not produce the entrepreneur. The man with the money does not always show a readiness to take chances. Similarly, the farmer who has not heard of the agricultural cooperative bank, the artisan who does not know how to borrow money to buy newer tools and increase his production, are handicapped and for all practical purposes either unemployed or, at best, underemployed.

By virtue of greater information, Kothuru has progressed. Today, Kothuru's residents are busy and move with purpose. They have little time to stop and wonder, but if there is something to stop and wonder about, they will ask questions, obtain the answers, and go about their business. For the resident of Pathuru, however, there are a great number of things he has not been exposed to; he stops and wonders at many things, but in the absence of ready sources of information, he stops for a longer time (he can afford to, for there is little that is urgent anyway) and wonders for even a longer time. He moves slowly in his daily work too, for it is the same thing he has always done, there is little that is stimulating, and there is little competition. If he is a washerman, he has his fixed number of families to work for; if he is a farm laborer, he has his fixed landlord. This attitude and the fixed nature of his duties have made him slow even to grasp at an opportunity when it does present itself. Some events, like the construction of the new bund some five miles from the village, or the rare occasions when transplanting of paddy is being done by several landlords at the same time and the demand for labor goes up, rouse the Pathuru laborer from his lethargy, but the opportunities are not constantly growing. They come and go, and between spurts Pathuru settles back.

Kothuru has no such fixed patterns. It has broken the pattern, consciously or perhaps, more likely, unconsciously. It does not regret what it has done. It knows that people who used to farm exclusively have become contractors, opened shops, and taken to teaching, thus bettering themselves economically. Similarly, it knows that Harijans have become M.L.A.'s, teachers, and factory workers. Looking at itself today, Kothuru is conscious of this change and takes it in its stride. It does not take time off to question the merits of change. It must be all right if everyone is better off and no one is getting hurt in the process. The rich are becoming richer. So are the poor. Each knows that he needs the help of the other. The rich invest, the poor provide the labor; the investment pays off, so does the labor. The understanding that comes out of such mutual appreciation of functions may eventually lead to a new dignity for the working force.

The new roles created by new economic units, whether they are the rice mills or the tile factories, have made the caste system obsolete. This is common knowledge in Kothuru, although it is never quite stated that way. Somewhere at the back of its collective mind, Kothuru is conscious that it is only in the economic field that the caste system has broken down. It is still firm in the social arena.

Pathuru, on the other hand, continues to believe that occupation must be based on caste, although it finds that sometimes this is not feasible especially when a bare living becomes impossible unless one gets away from the caste-based occupation and works at something else. So Pathuru's residents have worked out a compromise. Virtually every resident works at his caste occupation and if that is insufficient, supplements it with work in some other occupation. But when asked what his occupation is, he invariably says he is a washerman, or well-digger, or priest, or farmer, depending solely on what his caste is. His identification is with his caste, whatever his occupation. Since he does do something his caste dictates, he is not entirely wrong.

The Kothuru resident, on the other hand, responds with his chief income-producing activity whatever his caste is. After asking each respondent from Kothuru his occupation, we asked him what his caste was. If there was any difference between the two, he did not fidget or offer any elaborate explanation. (See page 17 above, where the Kothuru residents' answers to census enumerators were obviously different from the answers given in the course of this investigation. The differences can only be explained by the differences in the environment in which the questioning was done — and perhaps also in the "official" or "unofficial" nature of the interview.) Kothuru seems almost to believe that caste is one thing, occupation another. If the two do correspond to each other, as they did in many cases, that is all right too, for the individual may not feel the need to do anything else when he has already built up experience in his present occupation. In other words, the caste-occupation break was no rebellion, no thought-out campaign, it was just another of the changes that had taken place within the community along with other changes as new ideas, new vocations, and new goods — and new people — came into the village.

Division of labor in Kothuru also followed the same pattern. As new work opportunities opened up, some seized them; as new political positions opened up, some shifted into these; each in his own way, each according to his interest and his ability, selected his vocation. This new division of labor has not occurred in Pathuru to the same extent. There is no specialization here based on choice as in Kothuru.

From the data obtained with our questionnaires, the caste-occupation relationship could be analyzed. For this purpose, we first used the major caste divisions of Brahmin, Kshatriya, Vaisya, and Sudra — and the Harijan — but found that this was not wholly applicable to the villages we studied, for Kshatriya (the traditional warrior caste) has virtually no meaning in the present context. In addition, some major subdivisions like Kapu (farmer) play an important role in Andhra. Therefore we had to take into account most of the subcastes to deal with the differentiation reasonably accurately.

The main castes and subcastes in Kothuru and Pathuru are shown in the list on page 82 (their general area of traditional activity is indicated in parentheses).

In Kothuru we were told that every caste had some members who had changed their occupation. The only exceptions were the Chakalis and the Mangalis. In Pathuru we were told that caste still determined one's main occupation even if, for economic reasons, one shifted into another job provided that it was "not too much below his caste." We used information gathered from our sample of respondents to check these generalizations. Our sample did not have representatives of all the subcastes, but the large majority were represented. We found 24 instances of caste-occupation relationship in Kothuru, 39 in Pathuru. There were 16 instances of lack of relation-

CASTES AND SUBCASTES

Kothuru	Pathuru
Brahmin (priest-teacher)	Brahmin (priest-teacher)
Vaisya (business)	Komti (business)
Kapu (farming)	Kapu (farming)
Velama (farming)	Reddy (farming)
Gavara (farming)	Kuruma (shepherd)
Yata (toddy-tapping)	Gaondla (toddy-tapping)
Kumara (pottery)	Kumara (pottery)
Kamsali (smithy)	Kamsali (smithy)
Chakali (washing)	Chakali (washing)
Mangali (barber)	Mangali (barber)
Madiga (manual labor)	Madiga (manual labor)
Mala (manual labor)	Mala (manual labor)

ship in Kothuru, only one in Pathuru. This single case of unrelatedness was that of a schoolteacher who was not born in the village.

The finding here clearly points to the pattern which is developing in Kothuru. A secular and rational division of labor based on interest and aptitude rather than birth and caste — one of the most fundamental of all indices of development — is well under way there. The knowledge coming in from urban centers where this division has already occurred gives Kothuru the new norms that it needs to adapt to economic and social change. The opportunities opened by technological progress and the need for workers to fill the new roles encourage the Kothuru resident to defy (or ignore) convention. When a few make the break, the rest of the community would appear to accept it and in many cases even follow suit.

In urban India today, some intercaste marriages are taking place. In Kothuru it is common knowledge that this is so. In Pathuru it is not. We inquired out of curiosity if any intercaste marriages had occurred in the two villages. In Kothuru we were told by many persons that there had been one such marriage but that the couple moved to the city. In Pathuru the response was not so calm. A young man had wanted to marry a girl of another caste after she became pregnant. Both were expelled from the village. This was some years ago and no one knew what happened to the couple. Our respondents were reluctant to talk about it.

Tradition and, therefore, convention remain strong in Pathuru; in certain areas this is true of Kothuru too, but people there are more willing to make allowances for some unconventional behavior, whether it is in the way one dresses or the things one talks about. When there is uncertainty about what to do or how to react, both Pathuru and Kothuru villagers seek advice. In the way they go about seeking this advice it is possible to identify some important differences.

Sources of Influence. With the assumption that in a traditional community influence is based on age and hereditary status rather than achieved status (through formal education or knowledge), a series of questions was asked of all respondents about whom they would go to for advice in matters ranging from health to politics. In addition, the behavior of individuals in the communities was observed. The elite were asked separate questions on their own influence as they saw it.

The importance of combining measures — questionnaire-induced responses and behavior — was brought home by one issue. When asked whom they went to for medical advice, almost all of Kothuru's respondents pointed to the doctor. But when asked why, a large number of them said, "Because it is free!" Under such circumstances, general behavior and the interpersonal communication content as well as patterns must be taken into account before reaching any conclusions.

A distinct difference in patterns of influence between Kothuru and Pathuru emerged. The traditional pattern has broken down in Kothuru to a much greater extent than in Pathuru. It must be noted that Kothuru has more readily available sources to which it can go for information or advice. For example, a primary health center with a qualified doctor is located in Kothuru; the agricultural extension officer is also easily accessible. However, availability of sources is not enough, by itself, to bring about changes in attitude.

While Kothuru certainly takes advantage of the available sources in certain areas, it does not do so in others. For an injection when in pain, Kothuru's residents go readily to the doctor. Immediate relief is their hope. But when the same doctor comes around to vaccinate their children against smallpox, the response is poor, despite the fact that they can legally be forced to get their children vaccinated. As in most other areas in which Kothuru's residents are conscious of change and show a readiness to take advantage of available opportunities — and even create opportunities, as in migration to the city — a certain amount of *immediate gain* seems to be necessary. When they are aware of this possibility, their attitude is one of ready acceptance.

The difference in attitude between the two villages, therefore, has to be measured by this yardstick of immediate gain. And measured thus, Pathuru still lags behind. Kothuru's residents show a readiness to consult with and follow the advice of the young pioneers who were the first to venture out of the village; Pathuru's talk is incessantly of the difficulties that its pioneers encountered. Kothuru's illiterates respect the knowledge of a twenty-one-year-old newspaper reader and go to him for advice on their family problems; Pathuru residents show reticence in this regard, preferring to go to the *patel* who has always taken care of their families.

The younger, better informed residents of Pathuru are still fighting to achieve status in the eyes of the older illiterates; Kothuru's have achieved it. Few people in Kothuru wait with bowed heads outside the gate of the landlord if they can talk to one or the other of the informed youth of the village. If, however, the older person (e.g., the *karanam*) is also informed and freely available, they will go to him without hesitation. Not so in Pathuru. They would like to ask the *patel* for advice, but he is not freely available, because he shuts himself in his house. So they fend for themselves, showing little inclination to consult anyone at all. Their problems remain and time alone can solve them one way or another.

A few people of Pathuru, however, do go to the city to find a doctor, to Ibrahimpatnam to consult the *tahsildar* (revenue officer), to a city lawyer for legal advice, or to a city mechanic to fix their oil pump. But these are the informed and the rich. For the poor, there are few sources readily available, and those that are available are not utilized for fear of the landlord who has always expected them to turn to him for advice, but who may keep them waiting days or weeks for a *darshan* (audience). Meanwhile they discuss their problems among themselves, making them bigger as they go along, for rumor compounds rumor.

The land redistribution issue is a good example. By talking about it among themselves instead of seeking some competent source of advice (e.g., Yerra Reddy, a political worker and newspaper subscriber who is an extremely well-informed young man), they have made a mountain out of a molehill. Today Pathuru reeks with unfounded rumors about the great land transformation and waits in vain for it. No such frustration dogs Kothuru, for the residents are ready to seek advice from the best informed sources within the community.

It may be interesting to check this over-all impression with the figures as they emerged from the questions on influence. In the prominant characteristic of the individuals sought out for advice, the villages differed as shown in the tabulation.

NUMBER NAMING EACH CHARACTERISTIC OF "INFLUENTIALS"

	Kothuru	Pathuru
Knowledge/ education	33	16
Age/ status	7	24

It should be pointed out, however, that the questionnaire failed to elicit frank replies to inquiries about influence patterns. One of the main reasons was that most respondents could not differentiate between true influence and formalized authority, whether in the traditional sense or the more modern bureaucratic sense. Also, the latent desire of the adult male respondent to appear self-sufficient led him often to claim that "I decide for myself" or "I decide for my family," even in cases where this was not true (as observed in behavior).

Therefore, much of the information on influence patterns had to be obtained from observation. A few of the answers to specific questions, however, proved useful, especially a question on farming. Pathuru showed a far greater tendency to seek the advice of the big farmer or landlord, even if he was not up to date in his information on new fertilizers or on plowing methods. Kothuru was more enterprising and many farmers sought the advice of the agricultural extension officer or went to some other farmer who had demonstrated his ability to grow a better crop than his neighbor. Usually such a farmer had more knowledge of newer methods obtained either from the agricultural official or from reading the brochures put out by the agricultural department.

On the basis of the total picture gained from all the questions in this category as well as observation, it is possible to conclude that knowledge and education, along with proven ability (irrespective of age) in any given area of activity, seem to be far more important characteristics for influential persons in Kothuru than in Pathuru, where many still look to the landlord or the caste head or some other traditional leader as the fountainhead of all wisdom, irrespective of the nature of the problem. If they do take their problem elsewhere, it is usually on the advice of the traditional leader. Only the few younger men were capable of differentiating between "influentials" on the basis of their abilities in specific problem areas.

The fact that Kothuru could do this in greater measure shows too that there has been greater division of labor there, in the sense that not only are there different persons of influence for different economic problems (agriculture, industry, business, etc.), but also that the economic, the social, and the political sphere each has its own set of opinion leaders. The *munsif*, for instance, is the undoubted authority on politics; the *karanam* and the young priest-farmer on social changes; and in the economic field, the number of opinion leaders is as great as the number of avenues for economic activity. But the significant thing is that the opinion leadership does not overlap. The *munsif* is the first to recognize that he is no authority on farming; the *karanam* likewise on politics; and so on. Mutual appreciation of leadership roles leads to greater cooperation and lesser factionalism than in Pathuru.

This change in influence patterns can come in various ways. As new information flows into a hitherto communication-poor and isolated community, and this information is used by the elite or the mass in the economic sphere, new opportunities for work are created. The demand for labor increases and wages rise. The recognition on the part of laborers that they are an important commodity raises their value in their own eyes. The landlord (for he is the one who has the wherewithal to start a new industry) is no longer the dictator, even if he still remains the most wealthy.

Political Patterns

Attitudes toward Power. Change in the power structure can come about through the political process. The traditional village, in which power has been passed on from father to son in the various leadership positions such as *karanam, munsif,* or *patel,* may find itself being asked to vote in a general or a local election. Depending on the attitudes of the residents, they may either continue to vote as the "big men" tell them to or, recognizing that the ballot is secret, vote as they wish. Which they do depends to a large extent on what they have been told about the nature of the election. But, at any rate, power gradually becomes an achieved status rather than hereditary.

Although it is perhaps slower, change in the power structure can come through the social process. Interaction with people coming into the village from other areas who do not have any fixed positions in the community, and can therefore be approached more readily, may put new ideas in the minds of at least some of the villagers. Also the relationship between these visitors and the landlord or other traditional leader is seen to have equalitarian aspects. Somehow the landlord after such encounters seems to be less of a "big man" than he used to look. The villager may react to this by coming to judge the landlord on his ability rather than on his status.

Whatever the process, power becomes a little less permanent as a village develops. It is challenged, however slowly.

In the traditional community power usually rests with a handful of men. In a developing community, however, a separation takes place and power can be achieved in any of several ways. The informed man can become influential irrespective of his hereditary status, the wealthy man can achieve a status whatever his caste, the popular person can become the elected leader whether he is rich or poor. While this ideal state of affairs may not come overnight into any community, a developing community must show some change in its power structure in comparison with the relatively traditional community.

Kothuru and Pathuru do show these differences. In the earlier discussion of the economic, social, and political structures of the two villages, some of the differences were referred to and it was noted that Kothuru shows a greater readiness to depend for advice on the informed, the educated, and the qualified person rather than the man who has age or status alone. Age and status are of course not barriers to influence if, in addition, the person proves himself informed and qualified. If a landlord, for example, actively demonstrates these other characteristics, he can still retain influence and power, if he wants to. But his power is achieved, not inherited. In such cases, the landlord himself is the first to admit that his influence is less than under a traditional system, for he depends on others to give him respect voluntarily; he cannot demand it. Where, however, as in Pathuru, the landlord continues to believe that he is influential because of his inherited status, he will be more apt to deny that his power has decreased or that his influence is any less, despite the political changes that have occurred in the outside world and despite the fact that some of these have been brought into the village in the form of elections and so on.

To study this aspect of the difference between Kothuru and Pathuru, we asked the elite in the two villages whether they thought the landlord's influence had diminished. Every single elite respondent in Kothuru thought so; in Pathuru three out of ten thought there had been no change.

Answers to a question about power distribution were even more revealing. While Kothuru's elite were unanimous in saying that it was wider, only two of ten elite said so in Pathuru. Even these two were expressing a hope, not a fact. But they did have reason to be hopeful. The last Panchayat election in their village had shown that the landlords were fast becoming unpopular (thanks mainly to Yerra Reddy, the political worker, and his handful of young supporters) because of their isolation in the midst of change and their unwillingness to actively bring about development in the village. Kothuru, on the other hand, was happy with its elite, who had adapted to change, who went around talking to the villagers, and who were doing their best to bring better facilities into the village. They relied on the support of the mass and the mass gave it to them willingly. There were fewer factions apparent in the village and fewer jealousies and suspicions than in Pathuru.

In this interaction between elite and mass and the nature of the interaction lie several other pointers to the relative advance that Kothuru displays. One of these is the awareness of nationhood.

Awareness of Nationhood. Awareness of nationhood is the first necessary step before an individual or a community can display any spirit of nationalism. In rural India, especially in the context of economic development and national planning, this awareness must first be awakened with all the resources at the country's command before the mass of the people can be expected to make the sacrifices necessary and to show the understanding essential for over-all progress. Kothuru and Pathuru represent different levels in awareness of nationhood and hence are at some distance from each other in spirit of nationalism displayed.

The broadening of horizon which has already been referred to has made Kothuru more conscious than Pathuru of its surrounding areas, be they district, state, or nation. Where Pathuru continues to look only at itself (with distaste) Kothuru has gone outside of itself and taken advantage of opportunities available elsewhere, brought some of them back to itself, and built itself up. The information it has collected and disseminated in this process has enlarged its field of vision. Where nationalism is concerned it is still at a very early stage; but Pathuru hasn't even begun to move toward that stage, except for a handful of informed and educated people. In comparing the two villages, therefore, it seems more useful to look at consciousness of nationhood than at the more sophisticated measure of nationalism.

Awareness of nationhood was measured through several direct and indirect questions, one on information level, another on national goals, and a third framed to test for empathy at the national level. From answers to all these and from observation as well as prolonged conversations with our respondents which gave us a key to their ability to think in abstract terms like nationalism and democracy, the final picture of each village's awareness of nationhood was formed.

The gap between the elite and the mass again becomes very clear. Every single elite respondent in both the villages was aware of nationhood. Among the non-elite, however, the difference between the villages was sharp. Fourteen out of thirty in Kothuru and only eight out of thirty in Pathuru could think or talk in terms of nationhood.

The potential for nationalism, therefore, is certainly greater in Kothuru. But first, Kothuru must find the leisure to think about politics. Right now, it is busy with economics. Pathuru, on the other hand, has not yet even entered the economic stage. If it should jump into political activity first, the situation does not augur well for economic development, since the political leadership as at present constituted is apathetic to broad-based economic development.

Knowledge of Government Plans. Since consciousness of nationalism is limited in both Kothuru and Pathuru, knowledge of national plans in the villages is also relatively low. Both these factors help explain the attitudes of the villagers toward the plans. The difference between Pathuru and Kothuru is one of degree only.

Kothuru has been exposed to the five-year plan more directly than Pathuru, through the staff and activities of the Block Development Office, Pathuru's exposure has been considerably less direct. Few in Pathuru knew that agricultural loan facilities, the visiting V.L.W. (village level worker), and compulsory and free primary education are all part of the five-year plan. These things have never been explained to them, and their own exposure to the media was so low that they had not heard of the plan itself. Kothuru's residents, on the other hand, interact far more frequently with government officials, expose themselves to the media in larger numbers, and have directly experienced better economic conditions. Thus they have been led not only to relatively greater consciousness of some government planning and action (even if they are not too clear about the details), but also to a consciousness of sharing in the progress.

To the extent that more people in Kothuru have heard of the five-year plan or its manifestations in specific agencies or programs (e.g., Block Development Office, subsidized fertilizer), more approved of the plan. Attitudes toward the plan also differed according to whether a given respondent had felt the impact of planning. Many respondents had not, even in Kothuru, where private enterprise seemed to have had a greater impact on the residents than government action.

In view of this, although a fairly large number of our respondents in Kothuru could talk about government plans and also about their own economic betterment, they did not speak about the plans with the same enthusiasm as they did about economic development in general. They seemed to feel that whatever the government was doing was not necessarily for the benefit of all, rather for the few. If they themselves had experienced economic progress, there were other reasons for it than government planning. In this attitude, Kothuru's residents showed surprising sophistication. Those who approved fully of planning were those who were closest to the plan's benefits — landlords who had obtained contracts, Panchayat members who associated with the Block Development Officer and his staff very closely, and a few young men who were highly nationalistic and actively political-minded. The tabulation shows the knowledge of government plans and attitudes toward them in the two villages. Among the Kothuru elite, it should be noted, all the ten that we interviewed approved of the plans; in Pathuru only seven of the ten.

KNOWLEDGE OF AND ATTITUDE TOWARD GOVERNMENT PLANS

	Kothuru	Pathuru
Residents who had heard about plans or planning......	34	17
Attitude of those who had heard		
Approve fully	14	3
Approve halfheartedly	16	8
Disapprove	2	6
Don't know	2	0

However vague some of the respondents in Kothuru may have been in expressing themselves about government plans and actions, there certainly was far more consciousness of government because of interaction with officials and also direct experience with some of the manifestations of planning. Few government officials visited Pathuru, and on the rare occasions that they did, they met only the few top elite. The elite did not pass on any information they received so that it reached the mass.

Identifying Channels of Communication

If the government is interested in having knowledge flow down to the mass, it becomes very important to know the channels which carry this information; it is important too that the channels carry messages back to the government. This feedback becomes crucial for the purpose of constant evaluation and assessment of plan effects, of public receptivity and public reaction.

The government servant could be far more effective than he is, if he but took the trouble. He ought to be trained to look for the proper channels and use them properly. He can bridge the elite-mass gap himself, but he can do that only if he feels that he is not "exclusive," that he is a servant of the people. Or, if his time is limited, he can act in such a way that he indirectly helps bring the elite and the mass together. To do so, he should understand the social, political, and economic structure in a village, especially the communication patterns. Above all, he should be able to locate the intermediaries. For they are the ones who expose themselves to the media and pass on information to the mass.

How can the effective intermediaries be identified? Influence can be separated easily from the traditional power position although, as indicated above, they can overlap. The intermediaries are the true "influentials" and they are the active information-carriers. For they not only seek information as a means of achieving their specific ends, but actively engage in passing on this information, and are recognized as knowledgeable, informed, and intelligent by both the elite and the mass.

On the other hand, not all informed people are information-carriers. Many of the elite are informed but they do not pass on the information they have. It suits them to keep this information to themselves. However, there are also elite members who adapt to changes more intelligently. The fact that they are already in power of course gives them an edge over any challengers. But they can foresee the challenge and arm themselves in advance by becoming information-carriers rather than information-terminants. They talk to the mass, become known as knowledgeable and helpful, achieve popularity, and retain their power. To the extent that these men interact with the mass as well as with any of the elite who may still isolate themselves, they too can be classified as intermediaries even though they are already in the elite category. It is harder to find a member of the mass who is an intermediary, although there are a few — for example, Erranna in Pathuru.

The following list, which emerged from the field work in Kothuru and Pathuru, may help in better conceptualizing the process. It must be remembered that people can achieve power in any sphere — economic, political, or social. Everyone finds that information is important and most people seek it for specific purposes. But only those who are aspiring for power positions, or actively engaged in retaining and enlarging the power they have, become "senders" as well as "receivers" of information.

Information Seekers

Those who are expected to know: traditional village leaders, caste heads, teachers, etc. (usually receivers)

Those who desire (or need) some material things such as land, work, tools (some receivers, some senders)

Those who are ambitious for political power (receivers-senders), economic power (receivers), social status (receivers-senders)

The traditional outcasts who want to belong and be accepted (receivers-senders)

Information Indifferents

The fatalist: the person who has no incentive whatsoever to better himself, even if he does not have enough to live on

The passively contented: the person who has enough to live on and has no further desires

The superior being who "knows all": the rich man who lives a closeted life and does not mix with the "stupid masses" at any level, except when approached as "the master"

Information Carriers

Those whose status is threatened, usually older caste and village heads (receivers-senders)

Those who have accepted change, usually the friendly elite (receivers-senders)

The young educated villagers who identify themselves with the mass, usually those who are crusaders for equality of opportunity (receivers-senders)

Rumor-Mongers

The illiterate and ill-informed "rebels" — the most dangerous element in the community, they are conscious of some change but do not understand it; they seek some personal gain (free land, etc.) without making any effort (receivers-senders)

In the four categories into which the total community is divided on the basis of whatever primary role individuals play in the information-flow process, clearly the "information carriers" are the most important. They are already very much part of the village; most people know them by name and by sight. Also, they already command respect — the friendly elite, because they are friendly and interact with the mass; the older caste head, because he is the caste head and has been caste head for some time, although some younger caste member is now trying to oust him; the young educated villager because he is educated and belongs to a "good family" (otherwise he would not have been able to get an education) and yet identifies himself with the "ordinary people" of the village.

It is only by living in the village that these people can be identified, but the length of stay need not be long. It would be easy to see, for instance, that the village Panchayat vice-president, a member of the elite, walks around the village and talks to everybody; that the young landlord, N. Reddy, sits in the *bazaar* at the teashop and talks to the grocer, the Harijan worker, and the Panchayat vice-president. We have identified at least two elite members who are friendly and who interact with people at all levels in the socioeconomic hierarchy, although their own information level may be low, especially the vice-president's. But if he is given information, he will carry it to others; so will Reddy.

Then we see Erranna, the caste head of the Gaondlas, who is seeking information actively and talking to all the young, educated newspaper readers. His own information level is high and he is respected in the village by people of all ages. We find that he is fighting back a challenge to his leadership by informing himself and passing information on to the rest of his caste members so as to retain his leadership as well as to improve the economic condition of his caste. It is easy to get into a conversation with Erranna because he is articulate and jovial.

A newspaper reader in a village is the easiest person to identify. He usually reads in the open where everyone can see him, or he carries the paper with him wherever he goes. It is almost a status symbol. If such a person is young and carries the newspaper with him, he is usually an information carrier. All we need to confirm this is to see whether others approach him with ease. If they do, we have identified the politically conscious villager who probably already has some wealth but freely associates with the mass. In Pathuru we find that A. Reddy and Suryam are two such men, both well-to-do farmers, young and educated. On the other hand, G. Reddy reads the newspaper, in his little shop, but few approach him unless they go into the shop on business. He reads in the open only because he has to keep his shop open.

We have, therefore, been able to identify several persons fairly easily as information carriers. If we stay to listen to the radio in the evening, we will find that all these people are there — and few others. We are now doubly sure.

If we now take a look at the list again, we find that in the category of "information seekers" we have some who are also receivers-senders. These are harder to identify, but if one is prepared to spend a longer time in the village, it can be done. Erranna's challenger, Naranna, one can see, is seeking political power and is an active communicator. So is the Chakali Jiddanna, who is well on his way toward regaining the high social status which he had lost several years before during the cholera epidemic when he was expelled from the village. The "outcast" Sitanna is also fairly easily identifiable. He has learned to read and write and keeps himself informed. He passes on information to his group which lives in the shacks at the edge of the village.

All of these and more can be identified by any trained worker in the village. Today, most government officials whose job it is to disseminate information in several areas approach the Panchayat president or the *karanam* when they enter a village, tell them what is to be told, and leave. We notice that in Pathuru neither the president nor the *karanam* has figured anywhere on our list of information carriers. So Pathuru lags behind. In Kothuru, on the other hand, the *karanam* will be identified as an information carrier, but not the president.

The need for training government officials and others to recognize information carriers in communities such as Kothuru and Pathuru cannot be overstressed in the context of India's rural development. If villages like Pathuru are to have as much information available to them as Kothuru, and without a waste of effort and money which India can ill afford, identification of the communication channels already present and proper use of them are essential.

CHAPTER 4

THE ROLE OF COMMUNICATION

SOCIETY, it may be said, is communication. In this particular study, two comparable communities have been investigated. From this has emerged a picture of the communication process and its relationship to development in the three broad areas of economic, social, and political change. The changes in these three areas, it has been noted, have affected the communication process; so too has the communication process affected development in all these areas. But it is now possible, with the total picture of the dynamics of change before us, to bring into sharper focus the role of communication.

It should be stressed that we are here concerned with the role of communication in *developing* communities. The broad functions of the mass media which have been part of communication theory for some years are not discussed specifically, although parts of them may be recognized in this listing. What follows, then, is a list of the functions of communication in a developing community, as they emerged from the study of two Indian villages.

97

Communication in the Economic Sphere

1. Communication helps a person find alternative ways of making a living.

It is through communication that a person gets to know of the availability of different kinds of work. Once he has this information he can choose between alternatives. Lack of communication, on the other hand, will force him to remain in his traditional occupation, whether he is especially qualified for it or not. This is not useful or profitable either for him or for the specific field of activity, be it farming or brick-laying. No developing country can afford to have square pegs forced into round holes, for this is inefficient and wasteful for the economy — not to mention the psychological effects on the individual and on a community, if it has a large number of such persons.

2. Communication reduces the pressure on land.

Information which helps people in the developing communities find alternative modes of activity and move into them automatically reduces the pressure on land — an extremely important prerequisite for industrialization and the transition from traditionalism and an agrarian economy to modernization and industrialization.

3. Communication helps raise a family's economic status.

When information about alternative income-producing activities is taken advantage of, persons who had been sharing the produce of the family's land will tend to move into other jobs or set up small businesses to cater to the growing needs of others within the community. This helps the individual as well as frequently his family (depending on whether he is the main breadwinner or one of the lesser members of the family) increase the income received.

4. Communication creates demand for goods.

As an isolated and self-sufficient community is pierced by communication flowing from the outside, desires are aroused. The demand for new things increases. Orally, or through the media, information is passed on, and often sought, about the price of a product or its availability. Efforts will then be made by individuals to obtain these for themselves or their families. The demand need not necessarily be merely for consumer goods; it may include such capital-investment products as fertilizer for the farm or an oil pump for the well. In either case, communication aids development, for consumption must increase before production can go up and capital investment increases both consumption and production in the long run.

In addition to fostering the innate desire to emulate others, communication helps people learn of the benefits of new products, whether they are purely consumer goods or capital-investment products. In either case, the incentive to obtain these goods — by harder work or by spending from one's savings — is increased. Since savings in the traditional communities commonly are in the form of "dead" capital, the using of such savings aids economic growth.

5. Communication motivates local initiative to meet rising demands.

The presence of a market for goods — even if it is at one's own doorstep — is made known through communication. This knowledge motivates sellers or producers to add to their stock or to change production methods to meet a demand and profit in the process. It also encourages others to start buying and selling or producing. The first steps toward entreprencurship are usually taken by traditional businessmen or wealthy landlords who can afford to risk money, but soon the motivation spreads and the entrepreneur class is extended as more information becomes available on markets and methods. This information is soon not only received but actively sought. Where the sources for such information are within easy reach, development takes place rapidly; where they are not, the process is a slow one.

6. Communication broadens the entrepreneurial base.

Steps 1 through 5 add up to communication's most significant function in a developing economy. It helps enlarge the base of the entrepreneurial class. Where the rich have cornered the business activities of a community, it helps bring in the less rich, and where a specific caste has monopolized the buying-selling functions through its traditional role, it helps members of other castes take advantage of growing opportunities, for information about markets and meth-

99

ods no longer remains a monopoly. The creation or development of such a base is essential to the growth of an economy.

7. Communication helps economic development become a self-perpetuating process.

Both communication and economic development, by helping each other in their growth, make the total process a self-perpetuating one. For with economic development, the mass media and the interpersonal communication patterns tend to expand, leading to a great widening of horizons, aided by education, travel, and the like, all of which are parts of the total communication network. The constant interaction of the two leads to steady growth, once the process has begun — unless, of course, other factors of one kind or another intervene. It should be obvious that sometimes communication of certain kinds can cause a depression or other economic upheaval; but within the context of economic development it is not our concern here to deal with such situations.

Communication in the Social Sphere

1. Communication aids in the process of status change from heredity to achievement.

The informed person has always commanded respect in traditional societies. This is clear from the status commonly accorded the scholar-priest and the teacher. However, information itself is in such societies almost monopolized by the few, whether on the basis of class or caste. The priest's son learns from the priest; the ruler's (or landlord's) son learns from the family teacher. Education is a "luxury" which only the rich can afford; it is a necessity only for those born into the exclusive teacher-priest class. But when communication channels are opened up (through a broader based educational system, mass media, better travel facilities, etc.), persons in the lower socioeconomic classes see an opportunity to enter the ranks of the "respected." As information becomes more widely available, some seize the opportunity and gradually gain a status within the community which they would otherwise have been denied (unless, somehow, they had acquired wealth). These persons make great ef-

100

forts to learn to read and write, or listen to consumers of the media and other informed people. They seek out information and actively engage in communication. Soon they are singled out by the rest of the community as "informed" persons and turned to for advice. At this point a change in status positions has occurred. Status is no longer hereditary only; it can be achieved through communication and personal relationships in which information level becomes an essential measuring device. Status positions are no longer the preserve of the fortunate few.

2. Communication motivates the illiterate to become literate.

When communication channels are opened and information becomes a status-achieving tool, reading takes on a far more significant role in the day-to-day life of the individual. In relatively illiterate and isolated communities, reading is, in fact, a status symbol in itself. With new opportunities revealed, the illiterate are motivated to become literate. Adult education classes are even voluntarily organized by the few enthusiastic adults. Unless this initial drive is immediately recognized and nurtured by the government or other social agencies, apathy soon sets in. If the first surge of enthusiasm is fully utilized, adult literacy can become easier of achievement than most people seem to believe.

3. Communication helps shift influence from age and traditional status to knowledge and ability.

With new information flowing into a hitherto isolated community, the traditional leaders can no longer be looked up to as the fountainheads of all knowledge. There are vast areas of human activity and thought which have not been explored within the community. This fact becomes known whether a person from inside the community goes out into some urban center or someone from outside comes into the community. The local people, therefore, have to look for other "informed" people.

The farmer who hears of better yields elsewhere can no longer rely on the "knowledge" of the village "grand uncle" who has always been the "expert" on farming. He would rather discuss his problem with the agricultural officer, if one is available, or the landlord's son who has traveled and brought back with him some new ideas on farming methods. If some younger person has experimented on his farm and got improved yields, he is then sought out not only because of his knowledge but also because of his proven ability. The source of influence gradually moves from the grand old man to the grandson or the nephew. Similarly, information about hospital facilities in the city and the free injections that bring immediate relief reduces the business as well as the influence of the herb specialist. Thus, information, especially when it is backed up with reports of results which are then conveyed to the rest of the community through indigenous channels of communication, brings about a gradual change in influence patterns, and the closer such information is to the needs of the community and the more immediate the relief afforded, the quicker the change. (For example, a health clinic within easy reach builds up its clientele in almost no time at all, because the feedback to the community from the first "experimenters" is quick and enthusiastic.

4. Communication forces the traditional leaders to compete for status retention and motivates them to acquire knowledge and adapt to changes.

Age and traditional status, of course, will not necessarily count against an individual. A traditional leader *can* retain his influence and even increase it — but only if he adds to his knowledge and his ability, in other words, if he no longer relies entirely upon his past. Social status in the developing community is something to be earned.

When communication begins to make information available to a broader section of the community and influence patterns are slowly being transformed, the traditional leaders have two alternatives: to attempt to retain their status in the social milieu; or to close their eyes to changes and hold onto whatever they have had, accepting formal deference but gradually decreasing interpersonal relationships.

If the first alternative is chosen — and usually traditional leaders would like to retain their influence — they are forced to seek new knowledge and keep themselves informed; they are also forced to adapt themselves to changes. If they do this early enough, they can become the true leaders of a changing community; if they do not, then they can at least retain some influence though other leaders will take their place in specific areas.

If the second alternative is chosen — and usually it is not a deliberate choice but an apathetic resignation or ignorant, reactionary rebellion — the traditional leader finds himself gradually becoming more and more isolated. Advice is sought elsewhere. If despite his own lack of new knowledge in a changing world, he insists on leading and taking decisions, he will lay himself open to rebuff.

In looking for effective communication channels within the context of development, therefore, it is foolish to rely blindly on traditional leaders, for influence patterns change rapidly. However, those traditional leaders who have chosen the first alternative continue to be extremely useful persons — for they have prestige backed by tradition and influence backed by knowledge and ability. The identification of such channels becomes very significant in the development process.

5. Communication helps in inducing parents to send their children to schools.

There is growing pressure on land and on traditional occupations like those of the barber, the washerman, the village smithy. It is through communication that information about alternative income-producing activities becomes known. In a developing community this is often news about salaried jobs or training facilities. The need for some basic education if one is to be eligible for such jobs is recognized. Parents begin to discuss the possibilities open to their children. Information about educational requirements and educational facilities is sought. Parents who have the requisite information often make great sacrifices in sending their children to schools in distant towns. Parents who do not have this information fail to encourage their children to go to school even if basic education is compulsory and free.

If enough information is available to a large proportion of a community, efforts are usually made by the residents to build the necessary educational facilities within the village itself. If such information is available only to the few, the children have to be sent to schools outside the community. Not many can afford this. And these children are usually trained to seek jobs elsewhere rather than work within the community and aid in its development. Dearth of information and the lack of a widespread desire to educate all children thus results in the educated young people going out of the village to work. This not only increases the pressure for jobs in urban areas, but slows down the development of the rural community. The wide gap between the urban and rural areas is perpetuated. Social change in such circumstances is painfully slow. Lack of communication also perpetuates the gap between the elite and the mass within the village, for education remains the prerogative of the elite.

6. Communication helps people find new norms and achieve a balance during a period of rapid change.

During a period of rapid change — and much of this is brought into an isolated community through communication — it is communication again which has to take on the role of teacher or philosopher. Where it originally stimulated and created stress, it now has to act as a balm and reduce tension. For if such tension is not reduced, the people in the community will tend to become anomic, and this state of mind, if continued over a long period of time, can be highly detrimental to progress. Changes — whether universal suffrage or vaccination — introduced or imposed by edict seldom succeed if they are not followed by social adaptation. It is communication which explains the changes and helps people find new norms. Change brings with it a questioning of traditional norms, some uprooting of age-old beliefs and practices in many areas of human behavior, including the closeness of the primary group. With mobility and change in occupations, the joint family gives place to the smaller family unit. The competitive spirit in "open" roles is introduced by technological and other innovations. It is through communication that these changes can be explained and the transition to "modernity" made smoother.

In this communication process, the mass media have their part to play, but interpersonal communication too becomes significant. The proper channels for specific purposes therefore have to be isolated and full use made of them. The agencies responsible for the success of specific programs of social change must recognize the importance of the available communication channels and be capable of isolating them for individual needs.

7. Communication helps bring about greater equality and a greater respect for human dignity.

As status changes occur with greater flow of information and it becomes true that one need no longer be born into a specific socioeconomic class to become influential or respected, traditional social hierarchies topple. All one has to do to gain recognition is to be able to take advantage of available opportunities — whether they are jobs or entrepreneurial openings. With people migrating to other places or occupations, the landlords no longer can take it for granted that the "serfs" will continue to work for them no matter how much they pay for their services or how they treat them. The man in the street is now conscious of other opportunities. The landlord, therefore, finds himself in a position of having to woo labor and keep his workers satisfied. Wages rise, with a money economy, thanks to contacts with the outside "world."

The individual becomes aware that he wields a new power, even if only once in five years or so — he has the vote. He is no longer commanded to do something; he is requested. He *is* somebody now. He can raise his head once again, not only in his own house, but outside in the street where the rich landlords may pass too. He begins to gain confidence in himself as a human being with potential for advancement. Others are conscious of this too — for communication has brought in new ideas and new norms and explained them. Traditional deference to age or wisdom or wealth will continue, but in a modified form. It will no longer be abject subjection but voluntary humility.

8. Communication makes cultural and social change a self-perpetuating process.

Communication and social change, interacting with each other as described in steps 1 through 7, make of cultural progress a self-perpetuating process. Communication brings in new ideas from outside, explains them, and discusses them within the context of the local situation. An amalgam forms by itself in the contest between tradition and technology, between the old and the new, and between the rich and the poor. However, the source, the feedback, and all the processes in between must be dovetailed effectively if this progress is to be a smooth and continuing one.

Communication in the Political Sphere

1. Communication helps in the process of power change from heredity to achievement.

Information itself is, in many ways, power. It is only the informed person who can take advantage of whatever opportunities are available. This is true in the political arena as in any other area of human activity; this is true in the developed society as it is in the developing society. In the developing society, it is the person who is informed and makes the fact known who achieves power as he achieves social status. If his interest is political, he will use information to gain political power. In the traditional society, however, it is not always so. Hereditary power is present, but in such circumstances the hereditary leader usually does not find it necessary to pass on the information that he may have even actively sought in order to keep himself informed.

Political change can be brought to the developing community by edict (as when the government introduces adult suffrage) or by revolution or by any other means — or by communication itself. As the members of a small village community begin to learn of the outside world, their own ideas regarding their village leaders begin to change. In electing their leaders, the informed man takes on greater significance. Social and political positions begin to be thrown open to competition. In this contest, it is the informed man who has the edge. Traditional leaders will find it increasingly necessary not only to seek information but also to pass it on to let the people know that they are informed. New ideas will now be proposed and discussed and the person with the greatest amount of know-how and capacity to converse and convince will eventually achieve power. Traditional leaders who insist on maintaining their hereditary power without making the effort to seek information and use it to inform others in the community will find sooner or later that their power is waning. They will either withdraw gracefully or find themselves beaten by their own incapacity to recognize and respect change toward a growingly equalitarian human society.

2. Communication motivates traditional leaders to defend their power by raising their information level.

The challenge from the younger, literate, and informed nontraditional leaders will almost necessarily force the traditional leaders to be active carriers of information. It is only by becoming such that they can hope to retain their power. They have the advantage of being the "incumbents," but must actively seek to supplement this advantage with the information and the intelligence and the energy of the "challenger." In this process, communication at all levels becomes crucial. Traditional leaders can no longer confine themselves to moving horizontally in the communication process; they must move vertically too. All of which will have its own repercussions on the social and economic aspects of the community's life — adding in their turn to changes in the communication process. The entire developmental picture undergoes slow but inevitable change, in which the elite, as well as the elite-aspirants, have their parts to play. If traditional leaders choose not to get into the "race," their power ends and disappears altogether in one generation unless one of the younger members of the family decides to work for a power position. In this case, the elder hereditary head will be able to help elect his relative as "successor" only if he actively engages in the communication process. In any case, he can no longer take things for granted — including his own power position in his community.

3. Communication helps the mass recognize their own importance in the power structure and acts as a stimulus to political participation.

Without communication, widespread political participation is a figment of the imagination. Phrases like "the political mind of India" (or of any developing country or community) are meaningless if political participation is confined to the few and the rest merely follow their leaders to the polls every five years like a pack of sheep. Democracy itself becomes a sham. In addition to helping enlarge the base of political participation, communication helps the mass recognize their own significant role in government. Communication helps them find out that a leader needs support and that it is up to them to give that support or withhold it. Their own sense of power is thereby brought home to them — whether it is in a democracy or in any other form of government. Public opinion is something to reckon with and communication helps the public recognize its own role (collectively and individually) in this interaction between power and public opinion.

4. Communication helps the government learn of the needs of the public and plan its programs.

Any responsible government depends upon communication to give it a sense of the spirit of the public before, during, and after the introduction of any new program. In the developing countries this constant feedback is essential for effective planning. Economic development requires almost total participation on the part of the public, and the government in power needs not only to inform the public but to learn of the public mood. In a developed country with an efficient communication system, a trial balloon may bring immediate reaction, but in a developing country this is not possible. Hence the government's communication channels have to encompass every variety of interaction.

What is true for the government in power is true for political parties too. It is only through communication that they can gauge public need and determine what promises will be effective at election time. Often victory may be just a communication channel away — whether it is in an election or in a government program.

5. Communication helps the public know of government plans and programs.

The political decisions of the people will depend on how much information they have on the activities of the government and on its programs. Within the context of their own experience and judgment, they will decide the fate of the government. The more communication, the better the chances for a rational — or at least broad-based — decision. In the absence of effective communication channels and their use, a few interested persons at the top can very easily decide the fate of a party or program.

6. Communication helps a community or nation achieve power through unity.

Communication helps to bring together people of various regions, castes, languages, cultural interests, or other potentially divisive characteristics, to form a unified community or nation. For newly independent nations, this function of communication is of crucial importance, because the newly won freedom usually releases destructive forces of factionalism. It is mainly through communication that these differences can be overcome and unity achieved for purposes of national development and of national strength.

Communication widens people's horizons in gradually increasing circles from village to region to state to nation. And nationalism is an important step in political development before a country can make its voice heard in international forums and take its place in the community of nations. The slower this development toward nationalism, the greater the chances of domination by some greater power, not necessarily through conquest but by surreptitious support to one political party or by other covert means.

Whereas a unified country can act effectively in times of crisis, a faction-ridden country will find itself unprepared and psychologically weak. In the development process, the need for cohesion is extremely important. Communication contributes to cohesion by interpreting one group to another, leading to a respect for diversity within a broad feeling of unity.

7. Communication helps bring about greater equality and respect for human dignity in the political arena.

As in the social sphere, communication opens up avenues for political activity to those who do not have the traditional or hereditary advantage of being born with a silver spoon or a hereditary "big stick." This, in itself, brings changes in human interaction, leading to a reassessment of the social structure. When the "big" landlord begins to appear smaller than most people thought he was, the first step has been taken toward equalitarianism. The big and the small are in the process of coming closer. At voting time, this point is brought home even more clearly. It is only a matter of time before the "serfs" begin to hold their heads up and discuss issues with the leaders in political meetings. They begin to develop greater confidence in themselves at chance meetings with village leaders. Communication, by informing the public of issues and candidates, plans and programs, narrows the gap between the leaders and the followers to a point where each respects the other, depends on the other, and, therefore, interacts with the other on a reasonably equal basis.

Especially for the followers, this interaction is extremely important, for it gives them a dignity which they lacked in the traditional society. Political aspirants, be they traditional leaders or new challengers, do not look upon them as robots to be told what to do, but rather as human beings who are to be requested and convinced.

8. Communication makes political growth a self-perpetuating process.

Communication and political activity, interacting with each other as described in steps 1 through 7, make political maturation and growth a self-perpetuating process. This interaction keeps the power struggle in a state of constant flux, thus making the government, political parties, and the public ever vigilant. Power itself takes on a different character; it is transformed from the traditional "permanent" type to a "temporary" status and has to be nurtured through constant effort. By keeping every agency in the power structure informed, communication energizes the apathetic, softens the diehards, and stimulates the in-betweens in a constant and cumulative process of political sophistication.

Whatever the form of government, communication helps influence (and sometimes mold) public opinion and as public opinion begins really to reflect the "public mind," a traditional society has made the transition to "modernity" in the political sphere.

Communication and Development: A "Model"

"Societies," said W. W. Rostow, "are interacting organisms. While it is true that economic change has political and social consequences, economic change is itself . . . the consequence of political and social as well as narrowly economic forces." [1]

The role of communication in each of the areas listed above, therefore, is tied almost inseparably to that of at least a few of the other forces in the community. In this complex interaction, how can we sum up the contribution that communication makes? Also, how can we sharpen our conception of the relationship between communication and development?

We have noted that any development of communication and the resulting flow of information is followed by, or goes hand in hand with, development in other areas. Information of certain kinds, once released, awakens appetites for new things or for new ways of doing things. The nation's system, then, has to be ready to satisfy the new demands. The process also works the other way. Economic betterment and new knowledge gives an impetus to the acquisition of more knowledge and the communication process itself is aided in its development, through more buyers of the media, more travel, and the greater diffusion of interpersonal communication, as well as greater urbanization and education.

We may now attempt to sum up these relationships of development to communication in a traditional undeveloped village by drawing a possible model.

Communication, coming from outside, triggers change in a hitherto self-sufficient, closed economy. The information conveyed, if it is of a kind that indicates an economic or political opportunity, is first seized upon by one or more members of the elite. Communication, at this stage, still flows only horizontally in a strictly stratified society. Gradually, however, by a process of very slow diffusion through intermediaries who have access to the elite as well as to the mass of the people, it filters through to the lower echelons. If the communication is of a kind that fits into the frame of reference of the mass

[1] W. W. Rostow, *The Stages of Economc Growth* (Cambridge: Cambridge University Press, 1960), p. 2.

111

(e.g., land), certain ego-centered desires for economic betterment are activated. To what extent avenues are present for the effective channeling of these desires and their fulfillment depends on other factors in the community. Significant among these is the presence or absence of "dependable" and "disinterested" information sources, for any move made by the mass to act upon the information as originally received through the intermediaries may, at first, be killed by the elite in a desire to retain their political and economic power. They will do so either by belittling the importance of the original communication or by exaggerating the dangers of its possible effects, thereby arguing for the status quo.

A stress situation, however, has been created by the incoming communication. At least a few of the more adventurous people in the community will seek out more information, disregarding the advice of their elders who would rather "settle for security" under the all-knowing and powerful protection of the "big men" (the traditional elite). But if information sources are available for the young "renegades," change will occur fairly quickly, despite opposition from the elite as well as from the mass of the tradition-bound community. The time this change will take depends on the availability of "neutral" sources of information, whether they are visiting government officials, passing salesmen, or a publicity van of the state information wing.

If such sources are available and the communication channels are open, change takes place *in the same direction* for the mass as well as the elite (for both the elite and the mass will use the information), but, if not, change will take place *in opposite directions* (the elite will use it and better themselves and the gap between them and the mass grows wider). A by-product of the latter type of change is growing frustration and internal jealousies, leading eventually either to a fatalistic resignation out of sheer exhaustion or to a violent eruption.

In the "model" proposed, communication creates the stress by creating an awareness of the possibility of change and some of the possible rewards; and it is communication again which will provide the necessary information to release the tensions. If, however, we start earlier in time, for the purpose of building the model, other factors elsewhere will impinge upon the origin of the original communication itself. These may include decisions taken at some distant administrative center (e.g., land redistribution plans made by the state government), the transport facilities available for someone to travel to the village or from the village to the metropolis, the telecommunication network, the policies of the political regime, economic conditions (production of goods, etc.) — even on occasion such a mundane factor as fertilizer, which may be required for the village farmer to take the action desired of him.

However, it must be noted that the model is for the "hitherto isolated traditional village" and that it is specifically drawn from a communications orientation. Even in pointing out the "other factors," the relationship between communication and development is stressed. The model indicates the importance of the channels of communication in carrying the desires of those outside to those on the inside and the need for these channels to be kept open for smooth and early development. The feedback concept, it will readily be seen, is implied in the open channels. For demand and supply in the economic field interact within a communication system which carries messages back and forth.

If the "model" is now carried forward in time, the interaction will be even more apparent, both for the growth of the economic system itself and for the growth of the communication system. Their interdependence will also become clearer.

Once the needs are created and the ways for fulfillment of the needs shown, first the few and later the many will enter the economic field as active participants in an exchange of goods and services. Opportunities not only within the village but outside are taken advantage of. A developing money economy will make it necessary for new knowledge to be acquired both for immediate use and for safety (saving) and future use. Demand for items will create the supply and knowledge of supply will activate more desires. As jobs are sought and a whole new social process is introduced in a class- or caste-bound society, new roles bring their own adaptive processes, especially agricultural and mechanical skills. The information that is

113

exchanged in interpersonal situations in the early stages is gradually extended to the media-oriented, for with economic development and a growing money economy the media, as part of economic growth, gain their own consumers as a result of increasing literacy and new knowledge and new desires, imparting in their turn more information on investment as well as consumption. The process has, by now, become so cumulative that it would be impossible to separate cause from effect; it also becomes impossible to talk of communication, economics, politics, or social changes as disparate and isolable factors in the total developmental process. Each aids the other and each, in turn, is aided by the other.

Communication, however, remains an essential link and the purpose of the "model" is to bring it into sharper focus in the context of the developmental process.

"For continuous economic progress in India, Indians must be activated, which initially means the injection of a force for change from outside the more static setting. Government leadership needs to assume what has been called an intensive role, to operate its program in a way which will bring out the best efforts of most Indians." [2] Whether Malenbaum was specifically thinking of communication as an agent or not in this process of progress, an agent it most certainly is. And if the best efforts of "most Indians" are to be brought out, one must look into the villages, where most Indians are.

[2] Wilfred Malenbaum, *Prospects for Indian Development* (New York: Free Press of Glencoe, 1962), p. 322.

Appendix

HOW THE FIELD WORK WAS DONE

BECAUSE there is so little literature available on the actual conditions under which field work is done in the kind of communities in which we worked, it may be helpful to describe briefly the design of the study and the interviewing technique.

The Sample

Our experience shows that it would be almost impossible, and often undesirable, to expect to draw a fully representative sample. In most places the necessary data are not available. And in any case, there is a strong argument, in these cultures, for a purposive sample.

Our idea was to get a fairly accurate cross section of the population, but not necessarily an equal proportion from each of the categories into which this population could be divided. For example, two or three housewives could very well tell us the same story which twenty would repeat. But one landlord could not possibly represent six when five of them held positions of formal or informal influence and each had a distinct point of view. We therefore left ourselves open to interview any individual who seemed to be important in view of the responses of some of the early respondents. In the investigation of influence patterns, communication channels, and power structure, this approach had much to commend itself, for it was easy to foresee that we would have to pick our way back and forth through the maze of social relationships that make up an Indian village.

Let us take as an example a study of voting behavior. The largely illiterate and tradition-bound people of village India may not know until they enter the polling booth for whom they are going to vote, and after they vote, they may not always be able to tell for whom they cast their ballot. If we had asked such a simple question as "Can you tell me for whom you will vote in next week's election?" we would probably have ended up with ninety per cent "don't knows" or "undecided," whereas by asking half a dozen key individuals in the village what their political affiliations were and by observing the rest of the influence pattern, we could have come up with a much better prediction. In Kothuru, for instance, we could predict that a large majority of the population would vote, and that the vote would be for the Congress candidate. We could see that the *munsif* was extremely popular, that all of the opinion leaders were his supporters. We could see also that quite a large number of people were apathetic toward politics, but the efficiency and the enthusiasm of the "Youth League" members were such that they could round up enough people in the village (as they did for a single political meeting) to "get out and vote." On the basis of all these considerations, the prediction could be made with confidence. Without all of them, a prediction would be impossible.

These key individuals play the same roles in many other areas, including attitudes, behavioral patterns, adaptation to change. The sample, therefore, can profitably include a much larger proportion of the elite than of the mass. And by careful observation of the attitude of the mass toward the elite, one can gauge the effectiveness of the elite. In Pathuru, the top members of the traditional elite were effective only in certain areas; the younger elite were becoming effective in others. The mass attitude was ambivalent, but changing. Much, therefore, depends on some external forces (e.g., government action) and what form they may take. If these forces come into the village in a certain form, certain kinds of change would take place; otherwise, the results could be violently dramatic or pathetically regressive, depending almost entirely on a small group of the younger elite and their tenacity or lack of it.

An additional feature of the sampling technique was the "partial

118

interview" where we collected specialized data from people who seemed to be important sources for specific kinds of information but who could not be treated as full-fledged respondents for one reason or another (length of stay in village, frequency of contact with village in the case of visiting government officials, etc.).

The Questionnaires

The questionnaires, inevitably, reflected the total plan for the study. They were prepared in such a way that they not only allowed freedom to the respondent to express himself in terms which came easily to him (most of the questions were open-ended) but also left the interviewer enough scope to probe whenever a respondent became shy or defensive. The questionnaires did not have to be administered in one long session, nor did the questions have to be posed to the respondent in any set order.

The aim was to get as much information as possible from each respondent. Knowing the kind of communities we were entering, we could foresee that any fully structured questionnaire, administered directly, would be ineffective in eliciting opinions. We therefore went into the field with questions which grew out of hypotheses and had to be answered by all, but left ourselves free to ask them in any order and in the most informal settings possible. The idea was to make friends first, achieve rapport, get into a conversation starting from the respondent's family (an extremely important — and effective — opening device in rural India where personal questions are the easiest to get answers to) and gradually moving on to more abstract concepts. To aid this process, the questionnaires were constructed in such a way that each section could be separated from the others so as to fit into a running conversation, depending on what turn the conversation took. Also, the questioning could be terminated at any time and renewed later, because the respondent was not to be aware that he was being asked a certain number of specific questions. The questions were fitted into the pattern of conversation and terminated with the conversation, only to be taken up again at a later "chance meeting," which was "a friendship being continued and kept alive," for in the intercourse between respondent and interviewer each was a giver as well as a receiver. It was under such conditions that the questionnaire was to be administered and not in one formal and direct confrontation which would have thrown the whole effort into the wastepaper basket, for the Indian villager will refuse to be rushed, or if rushed, will refuse to open his mouth. He is not as research-conscious as the typical respondent in highly developed communities, including a few of the larger cities in India.

The original plan to make all questions open-ended worked extremely well. Although the Indian villager is not research-conscious, he is extremely friendly and considers it an honor when a stranger stops to talk to him. If, however, the stranger is curt and brusque and confines his end of the conversation to a specific set of questions demanding a one-syllable answer, the villager is hurt, because he is not being treated as an individual and the stranger is not really interested in his personal problems and ideas. But if approached through his personal problems and his family, he opens up quickly and readily. A question such as "Do you think life in the village is changing?" may bring forth a half-hour's discourse on how his grandfather lived, how his father lived, and how his children are living. The answer to the question, as far as the investigator is concerned, is buried somewhere in the middle of all this. It is the investigator's job to listen carefully and pick the relevant from the irrelevant. To the respondent, everything is relevant, because only through the past can he approach the present, and he can only do it by slow stages. He has not been trained to think quickly and provide the final answer without the preamble, which will also contain his personal philosophy. The investigator must show interest in the whole picture or suffer a "don't know."

The questionnaire was administered "indirectly" except in the case of the highly sophisticated and educated men (especially government officials and city-educated landlords who knew what research is) and those who specifically asked the interviewer to "take down" what they were saying. In all other cases (almost ninety per cent) the questions were asked with no paper and pencil in hand. Questions were asked and answers were remembered and put down in the respondent's numbered questionnaire at the earliest opportunity. The blank spaces were filled in after the next meeting — and the next, and the next, until all the questions were answered. More than one meeting with each respondent was inevitable; in some cases, this number went as high as six. For the purpose of observation and cross-checking in the total situation, this was an effective and by no means tiresome method, for each new confrontation could be a challenge for the interviewer who was drawing opinions from people who were supposed to be "incapable of having any opinions at all," or, if they did, of "articulating them."

Two main sets of questionnaires were prepared, one for the entire group of respondents and one for the elite only. In addition, several shorter questionnaires were drawn up for "specialists" like the schoolteacher and the postmaster who had specific kinds of information that we needed, and which others may not have had access to. These shorter questionnaires were prepared for the headman, the priest, the postmaster, the employer, government officials, teachers, the midwife, the political workers, the bus driver and/or stationmaster, the newspaper subscriber and/or reader, and the radio owner. In the field, a questionnaire similar to the one prepared for the employer was used for a technical instructor (carpentry center in Kothuru).

In using the elite questionnaire, those who were fairly highly literate and local leaders either for the whole village or for their specific caste or occupational groups were treated as qualified to answer the questions.

The villager, however illiterate or shy he may be, *has* an opinion. It has to be drawn out in a prolonged conversation which has some characteristics of probing, but this cannot be too overt. If probing is overt, the villager tends to withdraw. That is one reason why a long questionnaire cannot be administered at a single sitting or even two.

Opinions are expressed only in private — *after* some rapport has been achieved between the investigator and the respondent. The initial contact, therefore, is mainly to make friends. An example from Pathuru may make this clearer. Janganna is a Vaddra (well-digger by subcaste). He is perhaps the most disgruntled man in Pathuru. We met him casually and invited him to our quarters. He thought we were from the government and could help him get some land and/or some money to dig himself a well for his family and a few relatives living near his own little house. It took us an hour to convince him that we were not from the government. He then switched to a violent criticism of the local Panchayat and the landlords who controlled the money "which is ours." We went along with him just listening to his story. While he was at the height of his oratory, the vice-president of the Panchayat knocked on the door and came in. Janganna switched roles immediately, although the new visitor sat down quietly and asked Janganna to continue the conversation. But it was too late. The spell was broken. Two days later we visited Janganna at his well and he was again his normal self, for we were by ourselves. The total picture of Janganna's opinions, attitudes, and behavioral patterns emerged after we had talked with him five times, four of them running to at least two hours each. The fact that we

121

talked to Janganna was enough for the vice-president to bring in the subject of the well and the Panchayat's side of the story. We now had a more complete picture. Cross-checking incidents like this is not always a matter of chance. Often one has to bring in the subject indirectly into the conversation after picking an individual on the "other side."

Language is an extremely important aspect in such field work. Talking in the respondent's own language is almost a necessity. It not only helps in achieving rapport but often there are no exact equivalents for terms such as "equality" and "democracy" in the respondent's frame of reference even if the language itself contains words for such abstractions. However, if one wants to find out if the respondent is capable of thinking in terms of equality, it is no use pinning him down to a word. He has to express the thought in his own words. "After all, we are all human beings" may be his way of expressing it. But if we asked him directly "Do you think we are all equal?" he will immediately deny it because after all he is talking to a "big man who is city-bred, educated, and rich." He will answer, "No, how can I say that?" and pat himself on both his cheeks—a gesture indicating a "sinful thought" and pardon being asked of the Supreme Being through self-torture (hitting oneself).

Any "scale" used for such measuring of abilities to think in abstract terms, or even of attitudes, therefore, has to be subjective in the sense that the investigator has to assign a place for the respondent on any scale which he may be using, after a whole dialogue has ended. This is the way we used our "scale" for abstract thinking.

As for speaking in the respondent's language, one example may bring this home. The restaurant owner in Kothuru would not answer a single question when we first met him. We drank our coffee in silence, but we saw that he had a Malayalam (the language of Kerala state) newspaper on his table. We found later that he had come into the village three years before and had learned a little Telugu, but seldom talked to anybody in the village except his own family and a few shopkeepers from whom he bought some of his supplies. The next time we went to the restaurant we broached the subject of the newspaper and started talking to him in Tamil (a language which is very close to Malayalam). His response was most heartening. He was happy to talk in Tamil, a language he had not used since coming into the village and which was close enough to his own to make him feel friendly toward us. We did not press any questions on him and bided our time. Soon, he was coming to sit at our table to talk to us whenever we visited the restaurant. In six fairly short sessions, we had our questionnaire completed, including the fact that he was not really a Brahmin, but only posing as such in this village, so as not to keep high-caste people from eating in his restaurant — a secret which he knew was safe with us and felt free to share.

One last word about the field work. If one wants to be friends, one must live as the villager does — almost. If an investigator does not try his utmost to live on what the village has to offer, if he imports food and furniture, he is a "foreigner" (this does not depend so much on the color of the skin as on the sharing of the amenities as well as the inadequacies). It may be hard, but worth it.

Sample questionnaires follow.

A GENERAL QUESTIONNAIRE*

PERSONAL DATA:
1. <u>Name:</u> Satyam.
2. <u>Sex:</u> Male.
3. <u>Village:</u> Kothuru.
4. <u>Age:</u> 60.
5. <u>Caste:</u> Brahmin.
6. <u>Occupation:</u> Karanam since 1924.
7. <u>Length of stay in village:</u> Since birth.
8. <u>Size of family:</u> Wife and 8 boys, 4 girls (1 married).
9. <u>Schooling:</u> S.S.L.C.
10. <u>Schooling of members of family:</u> Six sons have been to school, eldest girl has gone to school, and third and fourth are going to school. Second girl not educated, but literate.

MOBILITY AND MEDIA PARTICIPATION:
1. <u>Travel outside village:</u> Rajahmundry, Bezwada, Vijayanagaram, Visakhapatnam.
2. <u>Frequency of contact with people from outside the village:</u> Surrounding villages; all visiting officials (quite a few).
3. <u>Visits to nearest city:</u> Once a month.
4. <u>Newspaper and/or magazine reading:</u> Was subscriber. Now that the library is here reads there every day (<u>Patrika</u> and <u>Prabha</u>). Magazines--only casual reader.
5. <u>Radio listening:</u> Owner. Regular listener. Mainly news, also music, also rural program.
6. <u>Movie viewing:</u> None in the last 5 years.
7. <u>Family members' participation in media use:</u> Wife illiterate. Sons read regularly in library, also radio, magazines casually. Wife listens to radio a lot (news, music, children's programs, and dramas).

INFORMATION LEVEL AND SOURCE:
1. <u>Have you heard about the following types of news?</u> †

Type of News	Where Respondent First Heard It	When Respondent First Heard It	Where Source Heard It	Discussion by Respondent with Others
Local.........	Somebody talked about it (the miracle) at home. Does not believe it is a miracle.	A few days ago (very next day after the incident).	From others coming from that area.	Discusses all the time with at least 20 people a day about all kinds of things. Mainly at desk on veranda of his house. Occasionally goes to junction--once in 2 days.
State.........	Hadn't heard.			
National......	Radio.			
International......	Newspapers.			
Science.......	Newspapers.			

* The questionnaire is reproduced here exactly as it was filled out in the field, except that Satyam is a fictitious name. At the end of the questionnaire is an account of some of the additional remarks the respondent made in the course of conversation. These remarks and the comments of the investigator about the respondent's personality have been somewhat shortened.

† This question, as indicated in Chapter 3, did not stand up well except in a few cases.

124

Type of News	Where Respondent First Heard It	When Respondent First Heard It	Where Source Heard It	Discussion by Respondent with Others
Economic.....	In town when he visits insurance companies and the staff talks to him.			Has advised others to take up insurance. But he is old. His son has taken insurance. Knows it is good.

2. Do you usually discuss the news with your friends? How often and with whom? Discusses with a number of people, mostly general news--local, national, and political. (Popular karanam.) Talks to whoever comes to see him. Also at junction.
3. Type of news that interests respondent: Public affairs and national news.
4. Why? Just general interest. Also village welfare--but not only village affairs.

INFLUENCE:
1. Do people come to you for advice on any topics? If so, which topics? Who comes to you for advice?

Topic	Who	Age
Medical......................	None.	
Farming or occupational......	Mostly farming. Also younger karanams from other villages. Mainly farmers.	Old and young. (Because of faith.)
Business.....................	For taxes, etc.	Old and young.
Marketing....................	None.	
Family's future..............	Mainly farmers.	Old and young.
Politics (voting)............	Only during election time. Mainly farmers. In this case also surrounding villagers ask him because this is main village in area.	Old and young.

2. Whom do you ask for advice?

Topic	Who	Age	Why
Medical................	Doctor.	Younger.	Qualified. Immediate relief, also safer. The native medicine is not as effective, nor is it as safe as this.
Farming or occupational................	Agricultural officer (for farming). Superior officers, Taluka Office. Revenue officer. Usually senior karanam.	Younger.	Qualified. He has read and passed exams.
Business, money, etc...	Nobody here.		
Marketing.............	Nobody here.		
Family's future........	Nobody.		
Politics (voting)......	Munsif. Also visiting political workers (respondent cross-examines all candidates).	Younger.	Munsif is much more in touch. He knows much more than respondent.

125

EMPATHY AND KNOWLEDGE OF NATIONAL GOALS:
1. Is your income enough for your living? Because of a big family and few earning members, it is not enough.
2. Is life in the village happy? Generally the people are happier. But it depends on yearly crop conditions.
3. How could it be improved? Enough food and clothing must be provided. This can be done only through active help of the government. Individual initiative is limited. For the animal what it eats is strength. For man what he has is strength; that is, what he has put by, security: "To have is as good as to eat."
4. Do you think the present hardships are temporary? Definitely. Things will improve. (People are more shrewd. They will get shrewder and more intelligent.)
5. Reaction to "Maybe we should all put up with present hardships as part of a sacrifice in view of the nation's long-term goals": Yes. We have to. And we see things improving. Didn't we do so during the war and rationing?
6. If you were head of this village, what problems would you try to solve? Sanitation first, roads, then irrigation.
7. If you were head of the state government, what would you do to help this village improve? Health, sanitation, and welfare. Sanitation is as important as good food, to keep good health.
8. If you were the head of the national government, what would you do to help everyone achieve a better life? First the food and clothing problem, then the tax system and the income and revenue for development schemes.
9. Do you think our five-year plans are doing what they are supposed to do? Yes. It has improved the village. But it is not very concrete. People are not yet united. They do not cooperate. (But they can't give their time because they are poor. And the rich do not want to spend.)
10. What, in your opinion, are the national goals as now envisaged? Enough food for all and general welfare and education. Self-sufficiency.
11. Would you like to see our country become a modern industrial state? Yes, it would be good. Work for all. It would be good for the country.

PLANNING FOR THE FUTURE:
1. Is your income enough for your living? No. (See above.)
2. Do you save money? Post Office Savings. Also son has account.
3. If so, where? (See 2.)
4. What are you saving for? Family welfare. For any contingency like marriage.
5. If you are not saving at present, wouldn't you like to save?
6. If you were able to save, what would you save for?
7. What are you planning for the future for yourself? Nothing. For your sons? Education and jobs. Not farming. Once they are educated they cannot stay in the village. For your daughters? Marriage.
8. What do you want your children to be doing when they grow older? (See 7.)

INVESTIGATOR'S SUPPLEMENTARY NOTES ON THE INTERVIEW

Respondent's Remarks on His Reactions to Change

Fashion. "Today the tailor cannot make a shirt the way I want it. He laughs at me and says this is not the style. A shirt must have a collar. In fact, he does not know how to make one without it, the way my grandfather and father wore theirs and the way I would like to wear it to be comfortable. The tailor tells me to make myself a 'buss shirt' or some new-fangled thing like that. These fashions are the result of newspapers, magazines, and movies. The youngsters see the movies, the magazine pictures and newspaper accounts of fashions

126

(and news pictures) and want to dress that way. They want to use the powders and the creams advertised, and so on. We older people have no voice in this any more. If we try to stop the youngsters, they will tell us we are archaic, or if we are firm, they will sulk, cry, and grumble. So why should we cause unhappiness? We know we are running against the current. So we give up. We want to spend our remaining days comfortable the way we are and not make things unpleasant."

Economy. "Yes, people are spending more. They want to buy all the latest things. Today they have cycles, but they are not content. My children are already asking for scooters. They want to travel faster. But are they prepared to work for it the way I and my forefathers sweated on the fields, to increase their yield and improve the land itself? No. None of today's youngsters can work a tenth as hard as we used to. Why? They drink coffee instead of eating a full meal in the morning and putting in a full morning's work. My children are not bothered about how I find the money. If they are prepared to work and earn, I have no objection to their spending the money on what they want. There is no question of saving. They do not think of it at all. They want to spend the money even before they get it."

(Throughout the *karanam*'s talk ran this theme of a passive, aping, consumer public, as against a creative producer public — whether in the field of fashions, in food habits, or in other behavioral patterns.)

Education. "Today the students seem to know only how to read but not how to write [again the consumer role]. They are not being prepared for their own day-to-day needs like adding bills or budgeting. Their arithmetic is hopeless. I have to teach my child after she comes back from school. I may very well ask, 'Why then should I send her to school?' Because of this impractical kind of education, many people who originally wanted to send their children to school (boys and girls) and even for higher education are having second thoughts. Some are beginning to feel that perhaps they should keep the children at home and prepare the boys for work and the girls for housekeeping."

Media. "Most of the change you see is the result of newspapers, magazines, and the movies — and the contact with the city (which is itself affected by the media). So, finally we come to the media all the same."

Respondent's Personality

The *karanam* was obviously an extremely popular man in the village, among all classes of people. Welcomes company and is freely

127

available. Also goes occasionally to the junction, being stopped all along the way by his many friends and acquaintances. Visits the reading room and does some reading there. Seems to have great faith in the *munsif* and the admiration is apparently mutual. Good sense of humor; very articulate and jovial. Although a Brahmin, entertains villagers of all castes who sit with him on the same mat on his veranda and talk as equals. Seems to have adapted to change remarkably well.

AN ELITE QUESTIONNAIRE

Respondent: Munsif (age 48, educated). Village: Pathuru.

1. Is life changing in the village? (More or less pleasant?) As it is in a transitory stage, there are some hardships to be faced--for the time being, of course. Comparatively, it is an uneasy period.
2. Do people ask or talk about their own plans for the future? Nobody has any plans. They only want to pass away the time. (What he means is the present.)
3. Is life faster? No, things are as they always have been.
4. Have you heard of the five-year plan? How does it affect this village? Fertilizers--more being used and encouraged. Oil engines are being supplied on loan. Subsidies are being given for well-sinking purposes.
5. Why do you think people are thinking more about economic development, etc.? (Use of mass communication?) All along they have been thinking of their own economic betterment, not of the country. Today it has not changed. They are not thinking more or less, but only of personal aggrandizement. (Story of husband, wife, and children in a boat. Wife asks husband: "If the boat sinks whom will you save? Me or the children?" He says: "Myself!")
6. Is there more political argument than there used to be? No politics at all. Only at election time, political workers come and cry something and gather supporters. But as for the local people, they have no interest in or knowledge of politics.
7. How many opinions in this village really matter? Is this increasing? There are about 10 people who express their opinions constructively (even if they are not practical). Previously only 2 or 3 people would think of village affairs. Not more.
8. Is the landlord's influence less than it used to be? Yes. Certainly it is less. In fact it is minimal.
9. Are people interested in more things? No, they are still limited to family and land, etc. They don't have the desire to know. And if they have the desire, they lack the sources of information, so they may give up.
10. Do people talk to you oftener about public affairs or international affairs? As far as the village is concerned, no.
11. Do you talk to more people than you used to? Due to lack of cultured, knowledgeable people we are unable to meet many people. And people may feel the same hesitation to meet us. So the answer is No.
12. What kind of people come to you for advice? Only farmers for their own affairs. That's all.
13. What kind of people do you go to for advice? None, except the Hyderabad doctor, when I have need, either for myself or for my family. In all other areas, I make my own decision.
14. Do you discuss any public questions at home? Yes, with my educated sons. The idea is to acquaint them with present affairs. And I have respect for their ideas and I want to know their thinking pattern.
15. How was the last election campaign conducted? Any change in the present campaign? No change has come in the public. So the same thing will carry on. Neither education, nor intelligence, nor literacy has improved. So how can changes come about? "Dabba lo vote veyyara ante veyyadame." ("One drops his ballot into a box because he has been asked to.")

129

A SPECIALIST QUESTIONNAIRE

<u>Respondent:</u> Midwife (age 21, educated and trained). <u>Village:</u> Pathuru.
1. <u>Have there been any changes in family life?</u> None. They live exactly the same lives.
2. <u>Has there been any improvement in sanitation?</u> It is a little better, because we have told them and they feel we may visit any time and inspect. So they keep fairly clean.
3. <u>Is there any talk or action on family planning?</u> None at all. Long ago somebody visited and told them. They have forgotten. No continued propaganda. So no action, no talk, only children!
4. <u>Are women's interests growing (public affairs, etc.)?</u> Not at all. Maybe in sewing. Predecessor taught a few. Others picked up from there. That's all.
5. <u>Is there any interest in news among women?</u> None at all.
6. <u>What are the reading habits of women?</u> Nil.
7. <u>What are women's attitudes toward sending children (boys and girls) to school?</u> Same as before. Maybe a few kapus. But women say they need the grownup children for work. "Is education going to feed us?"
8. <u>What are the women's attitudes toward sending children to the city to work?</u> Opposed. They want all the children at home. "Ayyo, ma bidda Patnam vellithe, evaru choostaro, ami chestaro." ("Oh, if my child goes to the city, I don't know who will see him and what they will do to him.") Only a few Reddy families (the rich only) are sending children to the city for education. One or two working there.
9. <u>Is travel among women increasing?</u> No increase. Some men go to the city a lot. But not women. Unless they have relatives to visit or children kept there for education.

130

Bibliography

BIBLIOGRAPHY

Books

Adams, Richard N., *et al. Social Change in Latin America Today: Its Implications for United States Policy.* New York: Vintage, 1960.

Agarwala, A. N., and S. P. Singh, eds. *The Economics of Underdevelopment.* Bombay: Oxford University Press, 1958.

Allport, Gordon W., and Leo Postman. *The Psychology of Rumor.* New York: Henry Holt, 1947.

Bauer, P. T. *Indian Economic Policy and Development.* New York: Frederick A. Praeger, 1961.

Beals, Alan R. *Gopalpur: A South Indian Village.* New York: Holt, Rinehart, and Winston, 1962.

Boulding, Kenneth E. *The Image.* Ann Arbor: University of Michigan Press, 1956.

Braibanti, Ralph, and Joseph J. Spengler, eds. *Tradition, Values, and Socio-Economic Development.* Durham, N.C.: Duke University Press, 1961.

Das, M. N. *Studies in the Economic and Social Development of Modern India: 1848–1956.* Calcutta: Mukhopadhyay, 1959.

De Fleur, Melvin L., and Otto N. Larsen. *The Flow of Information.* New York: Harper, 1958.

Desai, A. R. *Rural Sociology in India.* 3rd ed., Bombay: Vora, 1961.

Deshmukh, C. D. *Economic Developments in India — 1946–1956.* Bombay: Asia Publishing House, 1957.

Doob, Leonard W. *Becoming More Civilized.* New Haven, Conn.: Yale University Press, 1960.

―――. *Communication in Africa.* New Haven, Conn.: Yale University Press, 1961.

Dube, S. C. *Indian Village.* London: Routledge and Paul, 1955.

―――. *India's Changing Villages.* Ithaca, N.Y.: Cornell University Press, 1958.

Duncan, Hugh D. *Communication and Social Order.* New York: Bedminster Press, 1962.

Durkheim, Emile. *The Division of Labor in Society,* trans. George Simpson. Glencoe, Ill.: Free Press, 1949.

Epstein, T. S. *Economic Development and Social Change in South India.* New York: Humanities Press, 1962.

Frank, Philipp G., ed. *The Validation of Scientific Theories.* Boston: Beacon Press, 1956.

Galbraith, John K. *Economic Development in Perspective.* Cambridge, Mass.: Harvard University Press, 1962.

Gopalakrishnan, P. K. *Development of Economic Ideas in India (1880–1950).* New Delhi: People's Publishing House, 1959.

Haskins, Caryl P. *Of Societies and Men.* New York: Viking Press, 1960.

Heilbroner, Robert L. *The Making of Economic Society.* Englewood Cliffs, N.J.: Prentice-Hall, 1962.

Higgins, Benjamin. *Economic Development: Problems, Principles and Policies.* New York: Norton, 1959.

Hirschman, Albert O. *The Strategy of Economic Development.* New Haven, Conn.: Yale University Press, 1958.

Hoselitz, Bert F. *Sociological Aspects of Economic Growth.* Glencoe, Ill.: Free Press, 1960.

Hovland, Carl I., Irving L. Janis, and Harold H. Kelley. *Communication and Persuasion: Psychological Studies of Opinion Change.* New Haven, Conn.: Yale University Press, 1963.

Hyman, Herbert. *Survey Design and Analysis.* Glencoe, Ill.: Free Press, 1955.

―――, et al. *Interviewing in Social Research.* Chicago: University of Chicago Press, 1954.

Jain, Rikhab Dass. *The Economic Aspects of the Film Industry in India.* Delhi: Atma Ram, 1960.

Katz, Elihu, and Paul F. Lazarsfeld. *Personal Influence.* Glencoe, Ill.: Free Press, 1955.

Keesing, Felix, and Marie Keesing. *Elite Communication in Samoa.* Stanford, Calif.: Stanford University Press, 1956.

Khan, N. A. *Problems of Growth of an Underdeveloped Economy — India.* New York: Asia Publishing House, 1961.

Klapper, Joseph T. *The Effects of Mass Communication.* Glencoe, Ill.: Free Press, 1960.

Kluckhohn, Clyde. *Mirror for Man: A Survey of Human Behavior and Social Attitudes.* Greenwich, Conn.: Fawcett, 1960.

Kuznets, Simon, Wilbert E. Moore, and Joseph J. Spengler, eds. *Economic Growth, Brazil, India, Japan.* Durham, N.C.: Duke University Press, 1958.

Lazarsfeld, Paul F., and M. Rosenberg. *The Language of Social Research.* Glencoe, Ill.: Free Press, 1956.

BIBLIOGRAPHY

Lerner, Daniel. *The Passing of Traditional Society*. Glencoe, Ill.: Free Press, 1958.

Lewis, J. P. *Quiet Crisis in India: Economic Development and American Policy*. Washington, D.C.: Brookings Institution, 1962.

Lewis, Oscar. *Village Life in Northern India*. Urbana: University of Illinois Press, 1958.

Lewis, W. Arthur. *The Theory of Economic Growth*. Homewood, Ill.: Irwin, 1955.

Lionberger, Herbert F. *Adoption of New Ideas and Practices*. Ames, Iowa: Iowa State University Press, 1960.

McClelland, David C. *The Achieving Society*. Princeton, N.J.: Nostrand, 1961.

Malenbaum, Wilfred. *Prospects for Indian Development*. New York: Free Press of Glencoe, 1962.

Malinowski, Bronislaw. *A Scientific Theory of Culture*. New York: Oxford University Press, 1960.

Mamoria, C. B. *Agricultural Problems of India*. Delhi: Kitab Mahal, 1958.

Marriot, McKim, ed. *Village India: Studies in the Little Community*. Chicago: University of Chicago Press, 1955.

Marvick, Dwaine, ed. *Political Decision-Makers*. New York: Free Press of Glencoe, 1961.

Mead, Margaret. *New Lives for Old*. New York: Mentor, 1961.

————, ed. *Cultural Patterns and Technical Change*. New York: Mentor, 1961.

Mehta, Asoka. *The Political Mind of India*. Bombay: Socialist Party, 1952.

Meier, Gerald M., and Robert E. Baldwin. *Economic Development*. New York: Wiley, 1957.

Merton, Robert K. *Social Theory and Social Structure*. Glencoe, Ill.: Free Press, 1957.

Millikan, Max F., and Donald L. M. Blackmer, eds. *The Emerging Nations*. Boston: Little, Brown, 1961.

Mills, C. Wright. *Image of Man*. New York: George Braziller, 1960.

Muller-Lyer, F. C. *The History of Social Development*, trans. Elizabeth Coote Lake and H. A. Lake. London: Allen and Unwin, 1920.

Mumford, Lewis. *The Transformation of Man*. New York: Collier Books, 1962.

Myrdal, Gunnar. *Rich Lands and Poor*. New York: Harper, 1958.

Nair, Kusum. *Blossoms in the Dust*. New York: Frederick A. Praeger, 1962.

Park, Richard L., and Irene Tinker, eds. *Leadership and Political Institutions in India*. Princeton, N.J.: Princeton University Press, 1959.

Rao, A. V. Raman. *Economic Development of Andhra Pradesh 1766–1957*. Bombay: Popular Book Depot, 1958.

Rao, L. S. Madhava. *Panchayat Samithis and Zilla Parishads in Andhra Pradesh*. Hyderabad: Intekhab Press, 1960.

Rogers, Everett M. *Diffusion of Innovations*. New York: Free Press of Glencoe, 1962.

Rostow, W. W. *The Stages of Economic Growth*. Cambridge: Cambridge University Press, 1960.

Schramm, Wilbur, ed. *Mass Communications*. 2nd ed. Urbana: University of Illinois Press, 1960.

135

————. *The Process and Effects of Mass Communication*. Urbana: University of Illinois Press, 1954.

Schumpeter, J. A. *The Theory of Economic Development*, trans. R. Opie. Cambridge, Mass.: Harvard University Press, 1934.

Shannon, Lyle W., ed. *Underdeveloped Areas*. New York: Harper, 1957.

Shapiro, Harry L., ed. *Man, Culture, and Society*. New York: Oxford University Press, 1960.

Shils, Edward. *The Intellectual between Tradition and Modernity: The Indian Situation*. The Hague: Mouton and Co., 1961.

Singer, Milton, ed. *Traditional India: Structure and Change*. Philadelphia: American Folklore Society, 1959.

Spicer, Edward H., ed. *Human Problems in Technological Change*. New York: Russell Sage Foundation, 1952.

Srinivasaraghavan, T. *Modern Economic History of India*. Madras: Macmillan, 1958.

Staley, Eugene. *The Future of the Underdeveloped Countries*. Rev. ed. New York: Frederick A. Praeger, 1961.

Stouffer, Samuel A. *Social Research to Test Ideas*. New York: Free Press of Glencoe, 1962.

Tawney, R. H. *The Acquisitive Society*. New York: Harcourt, Brace, 1948.

Tax, Sol, ed. *Anthropology Today*. Chicago: University of Chicago Press, 1962.

Vidich, Arthur J., and Joseph Bensman. *Small Town in Mass Society: Class, Power and Religion in a Rural Community*. New York: Doubleday Anchor, 1960.

Ward, Barbara. *India and the West*. New York: Norton, 1961.

Weber, Max. *The Protestant Ethic and the Spirit of Capitalism,* trans. T. Parsons. New York: Scribner, 1930.

————. *The Theory of Social and Economic Organization*, trans. A. M. Henderson and T. Parsons. New York: Oxford University Press, 1947.

Wiser, William H., and Charlotte V. Wiser. *Behind Mud Walls*. New York: Agriculture Missions, 1951.

Articles

Amundson, Robert H. "Population Pressure and India's Five Year Plans," *Review of Social Economy*, 18:161–177 (September 1960).

Beals, Alan. "Leadership in a Mysore Village," in Richard L. Park and Irene Tinker, eds., *Leadership and Political Institutions in India*. Princeton, N.J.: Princeton University Press, 1959.

Beers, Howard W. "Evaluation in Community Development — The Indian Experience," *Community Development*, 5:203–219 (1960).

Bhat, A. R. "Vernacular Newspapers in India," in UNESCO, *Developing Mass Media in Asia*. Paris: UNESCO, 1960.

Birmingham, W. B., and J. Jahoda. "A Pre-Election Survey in a Semi-Literate Society," *Public Opinion Quarterly*, 19:140–152 (Summer 1955).

Boring, Edwin G. "The Dual Role of the Zeitgeist in Scientific Creativity," in Philipp G. Frank, ed., *The Validation of Scientific Theories*. Boston: Beacon Press, 1956.

Brzezinski, Zbigniew. "The Politics of Underdevelopment," *World Politics,* 9:55–75 (October 1956).

136

BIBLIOGRAPHY

Damle, Y. B. "Communication of Modern Ideas and Knowledge in Indian Villages," *Public Opinion Quarterly*, 20:257–270 (Fall 1956).

Desai, A. R. "Sociological Analysis of India," in A. R. Desai, *Rural Sociology in India*. 3rd ed. Bombay: Vora, 1961.

Deutschmann, Paul J. "The Mass Media in an Underdeveloped Village," *Journalism Quarterly*, 40:27–35 (Winter 1963).

Dube, S. C. "Some Problems of Communication in Rural Community Development," *Economic Development and Cultural Change*, 5:129–146 (January 1957).

Eisenstadt, S. N. "Communication Systems and Social Structure: An Exploratory Comparative Study," *Public Opinion Quarterly*, 19:153–167 (Summer 1955).

Garver, Richard A. "Communication Problems of Underdevelopment: Cheju-Do, Korea, 1962," *Public Opinion Quarterly*, 26:613–625 (Winter 1962).

Glock, Charles Y. "The Comparative Study of Communications and Opinion Formation," *Public Opinion Quarterly*, Special Issue on Communication Research, Winter 1952–1953, pp. 512–523.

Gompertz, Kenneth. "The Relation of Empathy to Effective Communication," *Journalism Quarterly*, 37:533–546 (Fall 1960).

Hirabayashi, Gordon K., and M. Fathalla El Khatib. "Communication and Political Awareness in the Villages of Egypt," *Public Opinion Quarterly*, 22:357–363 (Fall 1958).

Hoselitz, Bert F. "Problems of Adapting and Communicating Modern Techniques to Less Developed Areas," in Lyle W. Shannon, ed., *Underdeveloped Areas*. New York: Harper, 1957.

————. "Tradition and Economic Growth," in Ralph Braibanti and Joseph J. Spengler, eds., *Tradition, Values, and Socio-Economic Development*. Durham, N.C.: Duke University Press, 1961.

Katz, Daniel. "Psychological Barriers to Communication," in Wilbur Schramm, *Mass Communications*. 2nd ed. Urbana: University of Illinois Press, 1960.

Krech, David, and Richard S. Crutchfield. "Perceiving the World," in Wilbur Schramm. *The Process and Effects of Mass Communication*. Urbana: University of Illinois Press, 1954.

Larsen, Otto, and Richard J. Hill. "Social Structure and Inter-Personal Communication," *American Journal of Sociology*, 63:497–505 (March 1958).

Lasswell, Harold D. "Strategies of Inquiry: The Rational Use of Observation," in Daniel Lerner, ed., *The Human Meaning of the Social Sciences*. New York: Meridian Books, 1959.

————. "The Structure and Function of Communication in Society," in Lyman Bryson, ed., *The Communication of Ideas*. New York: Harper, 1948.

Lazarsfeld, Paul F. "The Prognosis for International Communications Research," *Public Opinion Quarterly*, 16:481–490 (Winter 1952–1953).

Lazarsfeld, Paul F., and Allen H. Barton. "Qualitative Measurement in the Social Sciences: Classification, Typologies and Indices," in Daniel Lerner, and Harold D. Lasswell, eds., *The Policy Sciences*. Stanford, Calif.: Stanford University Press, 1951.

————. "Some General Principles of Questionnaire Classification," in Paul F. Lazarsfeld, and M. Rosenberg, *The Language of Social Research*. Glencoe, Ill.: Free Press, 1956.

137

McCormack, William C. "Mysore Villager's View of Change," *Economic Development and Cultural Change*, 5:257–262 (April 1957).

Mandelbaum, David G. "The World and the World View of the Kota," in McKim Marriot, ed., *Village India: Studies in the Little Community*. Chicago: University of Chicago Press, 1955.

Mannheim, Karl. "The Positive Role of the Sociology of Knowledge," in Talcott Parsons, *et al.*, eds., *Theories of Society*. New York: Free Press of Glencoe, 1961.

Marriot, McKim. "Little Communities in an Indigenous Civilization," in McKim Marriot, ed., *Village India: Studies in the Little Community*. Chicago: University of Chicago Press, 1955.

Mathur, J. C. "Radio Programming and Programme Exchange in South East Asia," in UNESCO, *Developing Mass Media in Asia*. Paris: UNESCO, 1955.

Mead, Margaret. "Some Cultural Approaches to Communication Problems," in Wilbur Schramm, ed., *Mass Communications*. 2nd ed. Urbana: University of Illinois Press, 1960.

Neurath, Paul M. "Radio Farm Forum as a Tool of Change in Indian Villages," *Economic Development and Cultural Change*, 10:275–283 (April 1962).

———. "Social Research in Newly Independent Countries: An Indian Example," *Public Opinion Quarterly*, 24:670–674 (Winter 1960).

Prasad, Beni. "Influence of Modern Thought on India," *Annals of the American Academy of Political and Social Sciences*, 233:46–54 (May 1944).

Pye, Lucian W. "Communication Patterns and the Problems of Representative Government in Non-Western Societies," *Public Opinion Quarterly*, 20:249–256 (Spring 1956).

———. "The Non-Western Political Process," *Journal of Politics*, 20:474–478 (August 1958).

Radhakrishnan, S. "Culture of India," *Annals of the American Academy of Political and Social Sciences*, 233:18–21 (May 1944).

Redfield, Robert. "Relations of Anthropology to the Social Sciences and to the Humanities," in Sol Tax, ed., *Anthropology Today*. Chicago: University of Chicago Press, 1962.

Rudolph, Lloyd, and Susanne H. Rudolph. "Surveys in India: Field Experience in Madras State," *Public Opinion Quarterly*, 22:235–244 (Fall 1958).

Schramm, Wilbur. "How Communication Works," in Wilbur Schramm, ed., *The Process and Effects of Communication*. Urbana: University of Illinois Press, 1954.

———. "Information Theory and Mass Communication," *Journalism Quarterly*, 32:131–146 (Spring 1955).

———. "The Meaning of Meaning," in Wilbur Schramm, ed., *The Process and Effects of Mass Communication*. Urbana: University of Illinois Press, 1954.

Schumpeter, Joseph A. "On Capitalism," in C. Wright Mills, *Images of Man*. New York: George Braziller, 1960.

Shils, Edward. "Influence and Withdrawal: The Intellectuals in Indian Political Development," in Dwaine Marvick, ed., *Political Decision-Makers*. New York: Free Press of Glencoe, 1961.

Siegel, Bernard J., and Alan R. Beals. "Conflict and Factionalist Dispute,"

138

Journal of the Royal Anthropological Institute, 90:107–117 (January–June 1960).
———. "Pervasive Factionalism," *American Anthropologist*, 62:394–417 (June 1960).
Smith, Bruce L. "Communication Research on Non-Industrial Countries," *Public Opinion Quarterly*, Special Issue on International Communication Research, Winter 1952–1953, pp. 527–538.
Spengler, Joseph J. "Theory, Ideology, Non-Economic Values, and Politico-Economic Development," in Ralph Braibanti and Joseph J. Spengler, eds., *Tradition, Values and Socio-Economic Development*. Durham, N.C.: Duke University Press, 1961.
Stycos, J. Mayone. "Further Observations on the Recruitment and Training of Interviewers in Other Cultures," *Public Opinion Quarterly*, 19:68–78 (Spring 1955).
———. "Interviewer Training in Another Culture," *Public Opinion Quarterly*, 16:236–246 (Summer 1952).
———. "Patterns of Communication in a Greek Village," *Public Opinion Quarterly*, 16:59–70 (Spring 1952).
Tumin, Melvin. "Some Social Requirements for Effective Community Development," *Community Development Review*, 11:1–39 (1958).
Westley, Bruce, and Malcolm S. MacLean, Jr. "A Conceptual Model for Communications Research," *Journalism Quarterly*, 34:31–38 (Winter 1957).
White, David Manning. "The 'Gatekeeper': A Case Study in the Selection of News," *Journalism Quarterly*, 27:283–290 (Fall 1950).
Wilson, Elmo C. "Problems of Survey Research in Modernizing Areas," *Public Opinion Quarterly*, 22:230–234 (Fall 1958).
Wright, Charles R. "Functional Analysis and Mass Communication," *Public Opinion Quarterly*, 24:605–620 (Winter 1960).

Government Publications

Board of Revenue (Land Reforms), Government of Hyderabad. *Redistribution of Land in Hyderabad*. Hyderabad: Government Press, 1956.
Bureau of Economics and Statistics, Government of Andhra Pradesh. *The Economic and Statistical Bulletin*, 5, July–September 1961.
———. *Statistical Abstract of Andhra Pradesh 1958*. Hyderabad: Bureau of Economics and Statistics, 1960.
———. *Statistical Atlas of the Vishakapatnam District*. Hyderabad: Bureau of Economics and Statistics, 1951 .
Department of Information and Public Relations, Andhra Pradesh. *Cottage and Small Scale Industries in Andhra Pradesh*. Hyderabad: Government Press, n.d. [1961?].
———. *Districts of Andhra Pradesh*. Hyderabad: Department of Information and Public Relations, Andhra Pradesh, 1961.
Department of Land Revenue, Government of Andhra Pradesh. *Report of the Land Revenue Reforms Committee, 1958–1959*. Hyderabad: Government Stamps Press, 1959.
Indian Council of Agricultural Research. *Farmers of India*. New Delhi: Indian Council of Agricultural Research, 1961.
Ministry of Information and Broadcasting. *Annual Report of the Registrar*

of Newspapers for India, 1961, Part I. New Delhi: Ministry of Information and Broadcasting, 1961.

————. *India, a Reference Annual 1961.* Delhi: Research and Reference Division, Ministry of Information and Broadcasting, Government of India, 1961.

Planning Commission, Programme Evaluation Organization, Government of India. *A Study of Panchayats.* Delhi: Planning Commission, May 1958.

————. *Approach to the Second Five Year Plan.* New Delhi: Government of India Press, 1957.

————. *Third Five Year Plan: A Draft Outline.* New Delhi: Planning Commission, 1960.

Royal Commission, H.E.H., The Nizam's Government. *Report on Jagir Administration and Reforms.* Bangalore: Bangalore Press, 1947.

Superintendent of Census Operations. *A Picture of Population of Andhra Pradesh 1961.* Hyderabad: Superintendent of Census Operations, 1961.

UNESCO. *Basic Facts and Figures: International Statistics Relating to Education, Culture and Mass Communication, 1961.* Paris: UNESCO, 1962.

————. *Developing Mass Media in Asia.* Paris: UNESCO, 1960.

————. *Mass Media in the Developing Countries.* Paris: UNESCO, 1961.

————. *World Illiteracy at Mid-Century: A Statistical Study.* Paris: UNESCO, 1957.

Village Officers Enquiry Committee. *Report of the Village Officers Enquiry Committee.* Hyderabad: Government Stamps Press, 1958.

Miscellaneous

Bose, Anil B. *The Content of Indian Films.* Lucknow: Lucknow University, 1959. Mimeo.

Fagen, Richard Rees. "Politics and Communication in the New States: Burma and Ghana." Dissertation, Stanford University, 1962.

Indian Institute of Public Opinion. *Monthly Public Opinion Surveys.* Vol. 2, July, August, September 1957, and Vol. 4, June, July, August, September 1959.

Institute for Communication Research. *Papers on Mass Communication in Asia.* Stanford, Calif.: Institute for Communication Research, 1960.

Mehta, Aparna. *The Role of Voluntary Associations as Media of Communication in Bombay City.* Cambridge, Mass.: Center for International Studies, MIT, 1957. Mimeo.

Schramm, Wilbur, and Gerald F. Winfield. *The Role of Communication in National Development.* Paper written for UNESCO, 1962. Mimeo.

Seminar (New Delhi), 34, June 1962.

Index

INDEX